Moon Spells

Unlocking the Hidden Power of the 8 Lunar Phases, Wiccan Magic, and Witchcraft

© Copyright 2021

The content contained within this book may not be reproduced, duplicated, or transmitted without direct written permission from the author or the publisher.

Under no circumstances will any blame or legal responsibility be held against the publisher, or author, for any damages, reparation, or monetary loss due to the information contained within this book, either directly or indirectly.

Legal Notice:

This book is copyright protected. It is only for personal use. You cannot amend, distribute, sell, use, quote, or paraphrase any part, or the content within this book, without the consent of the author or publisher.

Disclaimer Notice:

Please note the information contained within this document is for educational and entertainment purposes only. All effort has been executed to present accurate, up to date, reliable, complete information. No warranties of any kind are declared or implied. Readers acknowledge that the author is not engaging in the rendering of legal, financial, medical or professional advice. The content within this book has been derived from various sources. Please consult a licensed professional before attempting any techniques outlined in this book.

By reading this document, the reader agrees that under no circumstances is the author responsible for any losses, direct or indirect, that are incurred as a result of the use of information contained within this document, including, but not limited to, errors, omissions, or inaccuracies.

Your Free Gift (only available for a limited time)

Thanks for getting this book! If you want to learn more about various spirituality topics, then join Mari Silva's community and get a free guided meditation MP3 for awakening your third eye. This guided meditation mp3 is designed to open and strengthen ones third eye so you can experience a higher state of consciousness. Simply visit the link below the image to get started.

https://spiritualityspot.com/meditation

Contents

INTRODUCTION 1

PART 1: MOON MAGIC ESSENTIALS 3

CHAPTER 1: MOTHER MOON: HER POWER AND SYMBOLISM 4
    GREEK MYTHS 5
    THE MOON AND THE TRIPLE GODDESS 6
    THE FIRST TRIPLE GODDESS 7
    THE SYMBOLISM OF THE MOON PHASES 8

CHAPTER 2: LUNAR PHASES: WHEN TO WORK MOON SPELLS 11
    SPECIAL PHASES 21

CHAPTER 3: MOON SPELLCASTING: TOOLS AND PREPARATION 24
    TOOLS FOR SPELL CASTING 24
    PREPARING FOR THE SPELLS 32

PART 2: PRACTICAL MOON SPELLS 35

CHAPTER 4: LOVE SPELLS 36
    TIPS 37
    LUNAR PHASE 38

CHAPTER 5: FERTILITY SPELLS 42
    FERTILITY RITUAL 43
    FERTILITY SPELL 44
    FULL MOON SPELL 45
    SAFE CHILDBIRTH SPELL 47

CHAPTER 6: MONEY AND CAREER SPELLS 48

Full Moon Money Spell 49
Spell to Get a Job 50
New Moon Promotion Spells 51
New Moon Money Ritual 52
Ritual for Performance Reviews 52

CHAPTER 7: MANIFESTATION SPELLS 54

Full Moon Ritual 55
Water Ritual 56
Wishes Manifestation Ritual 57
Cleansing Ritual 58
New Moon Ritual 59

CHAPTER 8: PROTECTION SPELLS 61

Energy Cleanse Ritual 61
Protection from Enemies 63
Dark Moon Protection Spell 64
Black Salt for Spiritual Protection 66

CHAPTER 9: BANISHING SPELLS 68

Full Moon Release Ritual 68
Spell to Banish Negativity 70
Four Thieves Vinegar to Banish Evil 71
Spell to Banish Depression 71
Reflective Banishing 72
Spell to Remove Curses 73
Spell to Banish Danger 73
Spell to Remove People from Your Life 74
Spell to Banish Alcohol Addiction 75
Spell to Banish Negative Influences 76

PART 3: OTHER WAYS TO WORK WITH THE MOON 78

CHAPTER 10: MOON WATER, CRYSTALS, AND OILS 79

Moon Water 79
Crystals 82
Moon Oil 85

CHAPTER 11: MOON GODDESS RITUALS 86

Drawing Down the Moon Ritual 86
Invoking Artemis (Full Moon Ritual) 88
Full Moon Ritual for Diana 90
Wiccan Esbat 90

CHAPTER 12: CREATING YOUR OWN UNIQUE MOON RITUALS 93

Unique Full Moon Ritual 94

    New Moon Ritual 95
    Tips for Creating Your Rituals 97

CONCLUSION 98

HERE'S ANOTHER BOOK BY MARI SILVA THAT YOU MIGHT LIKE 99

YOUR FREE GIFT (ONLY AVAILABLE FOR A LIMITED TIME) 100

REFERENCES 101

Introduction

The moon is one of the most majestic objects in the solar system and has inspired respect and curiosity since the early days of human life. This big bright body in the sky carries mysteries and wonders that few can grasp, and its secrets could be the key to unlocking more than we could imagine. This is why the moon is considered sacred to many cultures, and there is a long list of moon Gods and Goddesses across many civilizations.

The different moon phases have made it an everlasting symbol of transformation and time. It has also been linked with birth and death, creation and destruction. This powerful symbol is another reason many cultures have deities associated with the moon.

This book will explore those lunar phases and how each can carry a wave of magic within. You will learn the spells that you can cast during the different phases of the moon. We will cover every step you need to take to conjure the spells you want and explain how you should pair them with the various lunar phases. This guide is ideal for beginners because it presents easy-to-understand tips and hands-on instructions on how to craft those spells.

If you've ever been curious about the other lunar phases and how they could affect spell making, then you have come to the right place. The information you will find here is up to date, and it contains real spells that you can try for yourself. There is no experience necessary when crafting these spells because everything you need will be outlined. All that is required of you is an open mind, and a willingness to try this out.

We will explore all spells, from love to fertility, and how you can craft them. We will also discuss the ingredients and the rituals associated with those spells. If this sounds like something you're interested in, and we are sure that it is, then read on to improve your spell-casting knowledge.

Part 1: Moon Magic Essentials

Chapter 1: Mother Moon: Her Power and Symbolism

You will notice that the moon is often referred to with feminine symbols, and there is an explanation for that. While the sun is seen as representing masculinity, the moon is regarded as the female manifestation of all things. Yet, despite it being a feminine symbol, any gender can associate with and relate to it. Mother Moon is not exclusive of genders or races, and she belongs to everyone.

As we mentioned earlier, many cultures have looked up to the moon and associated Gods and Goddesses with the power and energy that come from it. When you're performing a ritual or spell correlated with the lunar phases, you may call upon one of these deities. In this next part, we will explore the most common deities across various cultures and how people view those higher powers, given the moon. We will also examine how religions associate the moon with feminine energy and consider it a symbol of purity and womanhood. Despite the moon's association with the female menstrual cycle–which we'll discuss in a bit, not all cultures think of the moon as a woman, though the majority do.

Greek Myths

The moon has a very rich background in Greek Mythology. Selene was believed to be the Titan Goddess of the Moon. She drove her moon chariot across the heavens every night, marking the start of a new evening, and is claimed to have had a lunar sphere or crescent on her head as a crown. She is the sister of the Sun God Helios and Eos, Goddess of the dawn. In Greek Myths, Selene is said to have fallen in love with a young king called Endymion, and she bore him 50 daughters, another symbol of the moon's fertility and its association with the feminine archetype. Over time, another woman, Artemis, took over and became the Moon Goddess after Selene. Despite this, Selene has often been considered the personification of the moon itself.

Aztec

In Aztec mythology, the ancient Goddess of the moon was Coyolxauhqui. She was also considered the Goddess of the Milky Way. She is often depicted in Aztec mythology as engaging in a fierce battle with her brother, the God of sun and war. The battle always ends with Coyolxauhqui's horrific death, and her death is often re-enacted in ritual sacrifice across the Aztec Calendar.

Mayan

Ix Chel was the Mayan Goddess of the moon. She was sometimes portrayed as a young and sensual woman who represented fertility, and other times, she was described as an older woman who is associated with death and destruction. Ix Chel was occasionally known as Lady Rainbow.

Christianity

Virgin Mary is often depicted with a new moon, a symbol of peace and illumination. The relationship between Mary and the moon has always been interchangeable. The moon is thought of as an ancient symbol of Mary, the Mother of God, and Mary is a source of light herself, the Mother of God, who is also light.

Polynesian

Sina is the Polynesian deity associated with the moon, and she is one of the most popular deities of that culture. Some say that she resided within the moon itself, and she is the protector of travelers on the road at night. Hawaiian Myth has it that Sina used to inhabit the earth with a husband, but she tired of it, so she left to live on the moon.

Celtic

In Celtic mythology, Cerridwen is the Goddess of the moon and fertility. She was often correlated with knowledge and wisdom and linked to the underworld. She is now symbolized by a white sow in many tales and myths. The sow represents her strength as a mother, and her fertility. She is considered to be both Mother and Crone, and she is often associated with the full moon.

The Moon and the Triple Goddess

As we've mentioned earlier, the moon has often been associated with women and female maturity. The Triple Goddess is the perfect representation of that, and its partnership with the moon has been the cornerstone of several pagan religions. The Triple Goddess was highly revered in Neo-pagan religions and rituals, and she represents a trinity that is the Maiden, the Mother, and the Crone which are the phases of female maturity. Each phase is a separate stage of a woman's life, and each corresponds to a different phase of the moon. In modern pagan traditions (Wicca most of all), the Triple Goddess is the Horned God's female counterpart. But, in Wiccan groups, the Triple Goddess is the only deity worshipped.

The Wiccans view the Maiden as the young woman, virginal, who is yet to awaken. She is about new beginnings and trying new things and the enchantment that comes with that. The Maiden also represents the enthusiasm of youth and youthful ideas. This is why she is associated with the moon's waxing phase when it grows from dark to full moon. This stage and others are worn as crowns by High Priestesses of the Wiccan order. In Greek Mythology, the Maiden is Persephone and was a symbol of purity and the legacy of fresh starts.

The Mother, on the other hand, is maturity and growth. In Wicca and other modern Pagan religions, the Mother is the next phase of a woman's life, and it is one that each must reach. This is when a female gains knowledge and is filled with excitement and fulfills herself sexually, emotionally, and socially. This is also when she's fertile and fecund. The Mother phase is when a woman grows and becomes the optimal version of herself, where she is at the height of her power and prowess. This corresponds to the full moon phase. The Mother roams in spring and early summer, which are her domains. Just like the earth becomes fertile and green in those seasons, so does the Mother. Many Pagan religions and rituals do not see it as necessary for a woman to conceive to assume Mother's role. In Greek Myths, the Mother is Demeter and is the world's source of life and giving.

The last stage of womanhood and the moon is the Crone when a female becomes old. As a hag, the woman has wisdom and is the representation of the darkness of the night. She is also associated with death and destruction. This phase corresponds to the waning of the moon and the dying of the earth. The Crone's domain is winter and its cold, linked with death and the final moments of life. In Greek Myths, the Crone is Hecate, who is wise and all-knowing.

The First Triple Goddess

Diana is an ancient Roman Goddess, also known as Hecate to the Greeks, and is considered being the first of the original Triple Goddess by many. Diana or Hecate was thought to be all three divine Goddesses in one. She is believed to have been represented in triple form even in the early days of her worship, particularly Diana. She was considered Diana the Huntress, Diana as a representation of the Moon, and Diana of the Underworld to represent death.

Hecate was often associated with witchcraft in the early days. Several tales mention a group of witches talking about the Triple Goddess. Interpreting Hecate as the Triple Goddess, which represents the moon phases, has also been present for some time. A Roman Philosopher called Porphyry was the first to make the connection between Hecate or Diana and the three phases of the moon. He described the Goddess beautifully, describing the moon itself as Hecate and claiming she was a symbol of its varying phases, and her powers were drawn from the moon. He likened her three forms to the moon as a figure in white and golden sandals to represent the new moon, and he made similar parallels compared to the other phases of the moon.

The Symbolism of the Moon Phases

The moon's symbolism has been present for millennia, and its phases have been said to affect humans in several ways. Many cultures believe that the moon had a powerful effect on us and can affect human behavior. This is where terms like "moonstruck" developed, which is used to describe people who act strangely. The adjective 'lunacy' comes from "Lunar", Latin for Moon Goddess. In other cultures, individuals believe that the moon is a God who has the power to predict the future. For example, Japanese priests would gaze at a moon's reflection in a mirror because they thought looking directly at it would drive them mad.

The moon's different phases are believed to signify various things, each with a certain set of values and influences.

New Moon: This is the beginning of the lunar phases, and for that reason, since early civilization, the new moon stands for new beginnings. In several cultures, sentinels would watch out for the new moon to herald the start of a new month, and they would report their sightings so the lunar calendar could be planned. The new moon is dark, and this darkness represents a fresh beginning and turning a new leaf. It is time to pick yourself up and set goals for the future. This is when you can plan for achievement over the next moon phases.

Crescent Moon: Now that you have planned for the future and thought about your hopes and wishes, it is time to declare all those things. You get to declare your hopes for the new lunar month and wish for the best. The crescent moon represents femininity and growth and thriving.

Waning Crescent: It is believed that the waning moon signifies losing someone or something with a bad influence on your life, and it is associated with loss and letting go of things. It is also identified with latent periods and meditation. A waning crescent symbolizes getting rid of negative energy in your life and working on becoming better.

Waxing Crescent: This phase represents development and pregnancy. It's about growth and creative thinking. When waxing crescent, you need to think about solutions for the things that trouble you and try to outgrow them.

First Quarter Moon: One week after the new moon, we have the first quarter moon. It represents the importance of having a head start for facing and conquering the challenges you were not prepared for. It is also a symbol of the time to make impulse decisions and act.

Gibbous Moon: When it is this phase of the lunar month, it is time to take a step back and look closely at your life. What are you doing right, and what are you doing wrong? Are you happy? With the Gibbous Moon, you must think about your actions and correct course if needed, without worrying about what has already happened. This phase is also associated with adapting to your current situation.

Full Moon: A full moon represents power and purity. It is the completion of objectives and reaching the peak of your prowess. Therefore, the full moon represents the Mother. A full moon is also a symbol of manifestation for the plans and ideas you have worked so hard for. You might not immediately see the outcome you want, but you're getting there, and you're doing all the right things.

Disseminating Moon: This is the time of the lunar month when you need to be grateful for everything you have and all the intentions that have worked for you. It also symbolizes the importance of being hopeful for the future.

Last Quarter Moon: This phase is about spiritual healing and the advent of the time where you have to move on. The last quarter moon is when you need to let go of past pain and feelings that have caused you to hurt, whether that is toward people or things.

Balsamic Moon: In this final phase, the balsamic moon symbolizes recovery and healing. It is the time to yield and repose, and it is when you should stop reckoning and get in your way. It is time to be at peace. Avoid projecting and taking actions only hurting you. This phase is about stillness and being at peace.

Chapter 2: Lunar Phases: When to Work Moon Spells

Witches and sages have been using the power of the moon for centuries as they understand its immense strength and how they can harness it. They also understand how it can provide them with good fortune, guidance, and success with their spell work. Living your life by the lunar cycle can bring harmony and make you feel happier and more energetic. This is why you need to know the different lunar phases and how to use them to your advantage.

Delving deeper into the topic, you need to understand that you cannot do moon spells at random. Each spell needs to correspond to a certain lunar phase. This is why you always have to consider the moon's current stage before you do these spells. While we discussed an expanded version in the previous section, and the associated symbolism, we will discuss focused stages now. It is generally accepted there are eight main phases of the moon, and it is during those that you should work your spells. There are also special phases of the moon that rarely happen, such as a lunar eclipse, and advanced students of witchcraft can use those for more powerful spells.

You need to believe in yourself and your abilities before you explore these spells because they only work if you believe that you can channel them. As a general concept, before we delve into each distinct phase, know that each corresponds to specific magic that you'll be practicing. For example, at the beginning of a lunar cycle, there is the waxing period (which is defined as the point where the moon is getting larger and growing), and during this, practice positive magic to bring new and good things into your life. Different phases will have specific connotations, which we will explore now.

New Moon

The lunar phases begin with the new moon when it moves to its position between the sun and earth. We rarely see it because it's the dark side that faces us at this stage. Occasionally, it can create a solar eclipse, which happens when it blocks the sun's rays from reaching us, creating a shadow on certain parts of the earth.

This phase of the moon is ideal for exacting a plan or launching a business endeavor. You could also try to gain publicity or introduce your work to the public. It is also great for money spells that will increase your cash flow, and you could try other spells that would lead you to new venture opportunities. Love spells are also common during this lunar phase, and those related to travel and exploration. Remember, the purpose of this is to stop clinging to the past and focus on new goals and dreams. Concentrate on the present and the future with your spells during a new moon, not the past. It's time for magic to drive you to new ventures, rather than dwelling on old pain.

Spells you could try during a new moon include banishing, divination, any magic for fresh starts and new opportunities, self-improvement spells, and curses. The new moon usually lasts for three and a half days from its first appearance--which happens at dawn. The prevalent themes include beauty and abundance.

Speaking of self-improvement, a new moon is also perfect for exploring the darker parts of your soul and trying to manipulate them positively. Each of us has a dark side we often refuse to admit or confront, even when people call us out on it. This is basic human nature, wanting to keep our flaws and the dark sides of our personalities hidden and tucked away. Instead of suppressing those sinister parts yourself, you can use them for good and improve your life during a new moon. Look deep into yourself and find the flaws you know are there but keep buried. Are you good at seeing people's faults and insecurities? Train yourself to utilize that skill to look for people's qualities and good traits. Maybe you can talk your way out of any problem. Think of healthy ways to control that quality, like getting ahead in your job without causing problems or hurting people.

The last thing to remember about a new moon is how it is ideal for setting new plans for the future, as we mentioned when we discussed its symbolism earlier. Set short-term goals during this stage for the upcoming cycle. Plan it by month; how do you wish the next 30 days to look for you? What dreams do you want to work on over this next period? This is great for beginnings, whether it is in love or business or even a social quest.

New moon ritual idea: since this phase of the lunar cycle is about comfort and fresh starts, this simple ritual can be done in your home. Before you begin, you must make sure your space is clean and organized. So, start with decluttering to prepare for the ritual. You could light a candle or burn sage to set the environment, turn on relaxing music, and keep a pen and sacred paper nearby so you can write.

The second step of this ritual is connecting with the Divine energy source you relate to the most, in this case, Mother Moon, or any of the other deities that represent her. Call upon them and honor them in preparation. Now that everything is set, sit down, relax, and write down the details you want for your future and explore your dreams for this next phase of your life. Whether it is a job opportunity, love, or any endeavor, write it down. The next step is reading those desires out loud. This is a crucial step because knowing the things you desire to happen in life, and the feelings that overwhelm you during this step are important for the manifestation.

Finally, after declaring your wishes, sit quietly and meditate. Visualize your hopes and aspirations, becoming real and happening. This ritual can be done on your own, or you could invite your fellow witches to join you.

Waxing Crescent

This second phase of the lunar cycle is called the waxing crescent moon. This is when the moon travels east in the sky. You can tell it is the waxing crescent when you see a small sliver part after the new moon, and it seems to keep growing bigger every night. It is possible at times to see the rest of it, but it will be dark due to a phenomenon known as earthshine, which is when the earth reflects the sunlight to the moon.

In this phase, you need to focus on your intentions and the actions needed to make them happen. You could write down your objectives for the future and read them every day to remind yourself why you're doing this. The waxing crescent is a time of focus and discipline, and preparation for the next step of your plans. During this phase, the moon's glow and power grow, as do yours. So, you want to draw upon this lunar energy and reap its rewards and strength.

Spell work during this point usually focuses on positive energy, and the waxing crescent is ideal for attraction and protection magic. Potential spells here include protection, healing, wealth, success, friendship, luck, self-improvement, or inner beauty. You can accomplish much during this lunar phase, and it is a time for self-reflection and working toward your future goals and dreams. The waxing crescent comes about 3 to 7 days after the new moon, and its main theme is manifestation.

Waxing Crescent Spell Idea: you can try bath magic in this part of the cycle. You could use elements you already have, like water and salt, which are cleansing components that can be used in this ritual.

So, run a bath and add bath or sea salts, whichever is at your disposal. You could also light candles to set the mood and prepare the environment. After that, the ritual is as simple as taking a bath. While doing it, imagine all your intentions and goals manifesting before you visualize them. Also think about anything that might be holding you back and let those obstacles flow down the drain as you cleanse yourself.

First Quarter

This next phase happens when you see only half the moon illuminated. It is called the first quarter because, at this point, a quarter of the lunar cycle is complete. Depending on the world location, people might see distinct halves of the moon illuminated so you might encounter the right half, and someone else in another country might see the left half. This is a critical phase of the cycle, and much happens within it.

In the first quarter, it is time to face the obstacles and challenges in your path. While the waxing crescent was about self-reflection and pouring your heart out, the first quarter is more about attracting things to you. Focus on the elements that matter in this phase and on reaching your goals. The full moon approaches, and you have to be prepared. The first quarter is also when you make changes to your plan and work around any challenges you might face.

You need to use the first quarter phase to attract the points you want in life like friends, money, and love using spells. Other spells that work during this phase are mostly creative magic, including divination, growth, motivation, and strength. This phase's theme is luck, and it comes about 7 to 10 and a half days after the new moon.

First Quarter Ritual Idea: since the first quarter is the time to review your progress and face your journey's challenges, you can do a sacred water ritual here. To make sacred moon water, you need a glass of spring water, natural salt, a burned piece of incense. Add the salt and the incense to the water after blowing it out. Make two even glasses of sacred water, place them on your altar, and start the ritual.

Meditate and review your intentions to see where your journey has taken you so far.

Waxing Gibbous

This covers the time between the first quarter and the full moon. The word waxing implies that the moon is growing in size, which it is, while gibbous is to signify its shape, and that translates waxing gibbous to "growing shape". The moon's illumination keeps growing bigger during this phase of the lunar cycle until it is illuminated, which marks the start of the next phase.

Things should come together, and you should feel more energetic and chase after your dreams and desires. The moon's energy will guide you here, and you will see your hopes and aspirations come to fruition. You need to believe that things are working for you and good works are coming your way. Yet, this phase is also one of patience. Things will take shape, but you must not rush the outcome. Instead, focus on tying up loose ends and developing, so you can achieve optimal results.

Spell wise; the waxing gibbous is ideal for constructive magic that can nurture and develop that for which you have been working. You might feel exhausted by this point and low on energy, but you can harness the moon's power to boost your power and confidence. You can do health, success, and motivation spells in this stage, and growth magic. The best time to work on spells in this stage is between the hours 10 and 11 at night, when you will have the most assistance from divine deities. You can expect to see a waxing gibbous 10 to 14 days after the new moon.

Waxing Gibbous Ritual Idea: as we mentioned, this is the last phase before the full moon, so it is time to revisit your intentions. Read them out loud to the moon goddess and reaffirm them. You have already planted the seeds, and it is time to check any alignments taking place for your plan to work. This spell or ritual can help you see signs from the universe you are on the right path. You need to blend (clockwise) frankincense, 1-star anise, and two pinches of dried rosemary with a mortar and pestle. When the ingredients are a fine powder, ask the deities to guide you and the universe to give you clear and loud signs to influence you on your journey.

Full Moon

This phase is when the moon's face is entirely lit by the sun. A full moon happens when the sun and the moon are on opposing sides of the earth. Theoretically, the moon is fully illuminated by the sun lasts for a few moments, but we also say it is a new moon because it looks that way, although it really isn't.

At this phase, it is beaming with the most potent energies during the lunar cycle, and it is the time to attract all good things to you. It is also time to heal from past emotional pains. For many witches, the full moon is a point where most magic can be performed, whether it is constructive or destructive. You could banish unwanted energies and influences from your life in this phase, perform divination magic, and create protection spells.

You must prioritize during this crucial time. The moon's energies are peaking, and you cannot waste such intensity on minor spells or unimportant quests. You should focus on your most important goals and dreams and how to achieve them. So, use the full moon's strength for the things that matter in your life. Everything should work out in this phase, after the preparations and effort during the earlier cycles. During a full moon, you can celebrate success after finding love or getting the job you wanted. Yet, it might not go your way. Regardless of how it turns out, you need to accept it as what is and move on.

Remember that the full moon guides you in this phase, so your intuition is sharper than other times during the lunar cycle. So, be mindful of your thoughts and dreams and focus on the path you want to take because a higher power is guiding you. You can perform love and healing magic during a full moon, and divination, banishing, dreams, and spirituality spells. This phase's theme is power because the forces at work here are heightened compared to the other phases.

Full Moon Ritual Idea: this is the best time for divination and readings, as see the fruits of your labors when it is a full moon. It is also an ideal time for communicating with spirits and deities since the moon's power heightens your senses. This is why you feel energetic when it is a full moon, and you don't need as much sleep. Consider what you're willing to receive. You can sit with a view of the full moon and start the ritual. Focus your whole mind and soul on the moon, and keep staring at it until you two become one. In this deep meditative state, concentrate on your intentions and on receiving guidance from the Goddess. Did you get what you were hoping for? Then be thankful. If not, also be grateful and think about what you might change. After you're done, you need to ground yourself; eating something heavy helps here.

Waning Gibbous

Unlike waxing, meaning growing, waning means decreasing. So, the shape of the moon is declining here, and the illumination is receding. This stage lasts until the moon becomes half illuminated. The moon's energies repel rather than attract, which makes this the perfect chance to work on banishing spells and others to remove things from your life with a negative influence. You could also do spells to end toxic relationships or unsuccessful business endeavors. Spells aside, a waning gibbous moon is a good time to clean your living space, tend to the garden, and arrange your magical tools and objects.

Focus on the things stopping you from achieving your objectives in this phase and the elements that might be draining your energy. Take a moment to stop and think about your intentions and where your past actions have led you. Is this where you want to be? If not, what's blocking you from getting there? What has been the most significant influence over your life so far in your journey? These questions will help you think about the changes you need to make. The waning gibbous moon might also be a time to step backward and rest for a bit, as the moon's light is fading and surrendering to the dark of the night.

Cleansing magic is recommended here. You can do curse removals, cleansing spells, undo bindings, remove negativity, and spells to help you get the results you want. Know, though, that the spell work you do here need not be directed at a person or an object but could be applied to yourself. Instead of trying to banish a toxic lover from your life, try ridding yourself of your feelings for them or your insecurities and self-doubt. Empowering yourself might work much better than trying to influence others' actions, and it may also be more ethical. The best thing to do is to work on the negative auras surrounding you and your perceptions and doubts about your self-worth.

Waning Gibbous Ritual Idea: You need to write down a list of all your fears, troubles, and insecurities so you can do this ritual. Some witches take this paper to a crossroads and get rid of it, but you don't have to do that. You could instead burn it and, with that, surrender to the moon's power as you banish and relinquish those doubts holding you from moving forward and getting what you need and deserve.

Third Quarter

The third-quarter moon is the exact antithesis of the first quarter. The opposite half of the moon is illuminated. This is also the stage that marks that the lunar cycle is three-quarters complete and is about to end. This is another opportune time to tackle the obstacles and challenges in your way. This moon phase can help you plow through your roadblocks helped by the moon's energy.

You can use the third quarter to quit that job you've been hating and wanting to leave for months, make final payments, fire staff, get rid of things you don't need, and return belongings to their rightful owners. You could also use this stage to get support from someone who could offer you guidance, such as a spiritual advisor or a financial planner. Listen to what they have to say and follow their advice, because it might just be the turning point you need. Don't give up and keep working on your goals and meditate to visualize your dreams coming to fruition.

The third quarter is a good time to practice divination to see what the following month has in store for you. As the moon fades, use magic to get clear of the obstacles you're facing and get rid of any negative influences. You can use spells to get rid of addictions, diseases, ailments, and any off-setting emotions that might be stopping you from getting the things you want. You could also engage in protection spells, break curses, and do health and dream magic in this phase.

Third Quarter Ritual Idea: during this lunar stage, you can take a cleansing ritual bath while burning incense or herbs so you could cleanse what you need to let go of and release negative energies and banish harmful influences.

Waning Crescent

This is the final phase of the lunar cycle, and it starts when the sun illuminates less than half of the moon, which continues until the New Moon. You may also notice the effects of the earthshine during this phase. The waning crescent ends when the sun and the moon rise simultaneously, which marks the start of a new lunar cycle with a New Moon. Also known as the balsamic moon, the waning crescent is a time of restoration and healing. It is the time of the cycle when your energy subsides, shifting from dynamic to quiet and reflective. You can take this time to reflect on the previous cycle and what has transpired. Think about the things you learned and the changes that have happened. Take these lessons into consideration as you prepare for the next lunar cycle.

During this phase, banishing magic is considered at its most powerful. So, this is the time to get rid of anything troubling you, whether it is clutter around your home or heavy feelings weighing you down. It is also the time to end toxic relationships so you can focus on yourself and your recovery. Meditate and nurture yourself, and take this phase to recuperate, rest, and recharge your energy.

You can cast spells to get rid of negative influences in this phase, and spells to remove obstacles and bring you peace of mind. Use magic to tackle situations like divorce, separation, getting rid of stalkers, and protection. Remember this stage is about finding balance and slowing down to reflect on the past and resolve to help you move forward. Use this time to bid farewell to the things holding you back and no longer serving a meaningful purpose in your life.

Special Phases

As we mentioned earlier, there are special phases of the lunar cycle. Some of these don't happen every month, while others do. You must understand them and the magic you can practice.

Dark Moon: The dark moon happens on the eve of a new moon, and it is considered being the final day in a complete lunar cycle. The dark moon is often associated with darker aspects of the Moon Goddess pertaining to death and destruction, which is why it is ideal for destructive magic. You can do hexes, curses, banishing, divorce, separation, and protection spells. They are significantly more powerful if cast during a dark moon, amplified by this part of the lunar phase's power. It is better to channel these dark energies toward self-reflection and rebuilding. You can use this power to do healing and cleansing rituals. It's also a good time to meditate and perform divination rituals to try to get a glimpse into your future and see what awaits you.

Lunar Eclipse: Lunar eclipses don't come often, and it is a moon phase brimming with magical power, and you should never miss out on this opportunity. Lunar eclipses are often associated with change, and they symbolize major shifts in your life. Those changes can lead you closer to your goals and dreams. A lunar eclipse usually happens once every year when the sun and moon's powers connect and create harmony and balance between the female and male divine energies. This union between those two opposite powers can support you to do powerful magic that will allow you to achieve things you never thought were possible.

There are a few who believe that lunar eclipses are a manifestation of every moon phase's energies because the eclipse starts with a full moon that wanes until it goes dark. After that, the new moon's silver manifests, and the moon wanes to full again. So, it can be said that you have the energies of the different phases all at once. You can do all kinds of magic spells here, and they will be potent and powerful. Remember to keep timing in mind when performing rituals during a lunar eclipse because the phases will vary depending on where you're located. So, keep an eye on the local start and end times when you plan for this ritual. Spells you can do during a lunar eclipse include money, relationships, healing, wealth, protection, and divination.

Blue Moon: Whenever there are two full moons in a lunar cycle, the second one is called a Blue Moon. Some believe that the blue moon is much more powerful than a full moon, and it's used to do powerful and significant spells. A Blue Moon only happens every 2.5 years, and it usually falls on a different month every year. Exercise caution when practicing magic during this special moon phase because the outcome might be exponentially more effective than you predict.

Many witches believe that the Blue Moon is a time where the veil between our world and that of the spirits is very thin, which can facilitate any communication between both worlds. During this time, you will have heightened powers and clarity, and this is why it is ideal for divination. Your magic will be amplified, and your psychic skills will also most likely be at their peak. So, seize this rare opportunity to harness the moon's power and use it to your advantage. Spells and magic that happen during the Blue Moon often have long-term consequences, so always remember that and don't use a spell when you are not sure about the effects.

It is ideal to plant new seeds and ideas that could help you move forward toward your dreams because they will have long-term effects, and you will see significant changes in your life. Meditation is highly recommended during this moon phase, as is divination because of your heightened powers and abilities.

Chapter 3: Moon Spellcasting: Tools and Preparation

Spellcasting is an intricate process that requires an understanding of the world of magic, and more important, having the necessary tools to perform rituals and spells. For some, it can be an easy process, while for others, it's very complicated. In this chapter, we will cover the tools and items you will need to cast spells and how you should prepare. Once you grasp the basic objects you will need, and optional ones, spellcasting becomes more about the magic rather than scrambling to find the tools and ingredients. You need certain items you cannot perform your spells without, which we will explore during this chapter for moon spells. A witch will also need to prepare to perform these spells and ready her mind, body, and spirit to delve into the magic and spell casting, which we will also cover in this chapter.

Tools for Spell Casting

So, what is the point of these tools and items? Wiccans believe these tools are used in rituals to honor the deities and channel the moon's psychic energies to help perform a certain action. These are the most common tools that a witch needs to cast spells and perform rituals.

Altar

The first item we will talk about is a basic one that any witch needs to have. The altar is a sacred space in which you will store all your ritual tools and ingredients. More important, the altar is used as a workspace when you perform and make spells. Many people commonly use a table as an altar, but that might not be ideal if you want a mobile altar. Several witches use a portable case to use an altar, and they can store their tools and ingredients in something as simple as a drawer.

The importance of an altar extends beyond having a space to store your tools and perform the rituals. The altar is often used to connect with the deities who will guide you on your ritual, which is why altars have always been important in pagan rituals. People put so much emphasis on altars they have more than one at home, each for a certain ceremony or ritual.

There isn't a correct way to set up an altar; it's your magical space, and you can do with it what you will and set it up; however you please. Practitioners like to add decorative touches like a special scarf or cover for the altar. As for the altar's material, use wood, ceramic, or stone because these elements ground the energy, and you can also engrave any symbols or ritualistic inscriptions into them.

Altar Accessories

You don't just buy an altar and start performing rituals. You need to get the objects and accessories that are going to be using with the altar. This starts with candleholders for all the rituals in which you will light candles to set the environment and cast a spell. You will also need incense burners because many spells require burning incense. Crystals may be needed and vases for flowers. Some of these items aren't used for magic per se, but they give the magical items you do use their potency, and they also create a beautiful and sacred space to practice your rituals and cast your spells.

Athame and Other Blades

One of the essential tools for performing spells is a blade, commonly called an *athame* in witchcraft. It usually comes with a black handle and is made from pure metal; it is not supposed to be a knife to cut herbs or used as a regular knife, so it is not sharpened since it doesn't have practical uses. The athame is used to indicate directions, direct energy, and cut a way out of the circle safely without compromising your energy. It is believed this blade represents the masculine energy and the air element.

An athame might also be used as a wand. You use another blade to cut herbs, called a *boline,* which is shaped like a crescent moon and comes with a white handle. The boline is also used to inscribe candles. Sometimes, for more advanced witches, a sword is used to mark sacred circles of great significance and size. But usually only the high priestess of a coven may use it.

Burin

A burin is not exactly a blade; it's a small tool with a thin point used by witches to carve words and symbols into candles, wood, and other magical objects. You can make it out of whatever material you please, such as pins or nails or any other similar item.

Wands

A wand can be made out of any natural material, though it is most commonly made from wood, rock, or metal. It symbolizes the Air element, in some traditions, Fire, and it is often used to summon entities and invoke deities. A wand is also used to direct energy, bless something, and consecrate sacred spaces or magical items.

Broom or Besom

This is one of the more personal spell casting tools. You can have one custom made from the twigs of a tree of your choice or make it yourself. You don't use a broom or besom for sweeping and cleaning dirt; it is used to cleanse negative energies and remove bad influences, usually before spell work. To use a besom or broom, gently sweep the room in a clockwise direction, rid it of any negative energies, open the door, throw the energy outside, and close the door afterward. A lot of witches considered their brooms sacred, and many believe they should never touch the ground. Some use the broom or besom in seasonal fertility dances or with other traditions.

Bells and Rattles

In many ancient civilizations, hundreds of years ago, they used bells to ward off evil and dark spirits. The vibrations coming from a bell were also believed to be the source of great power. Bells were used to summon spirits, not just banish them. You ring a bell in the corner of a room to get rid of dark energies and evil presence. You can also use rattles and singing bowls to bring peace and harmony to a sacred space or cleanse a magic ritual.

Grimoire

A book of shadows or a grimoire is another important tool in a witch's arsenal. It is a notebook where you journal and document your magical practices and spell work. Each witch writes their grimoire, and it usually chronicles everything they've learned on their journey, including spells, rituals, invocations, moon charts, and a list of deities and pantheons. While the book of shadows is a highly personal tool that witches keep private and secure, it can sometimes be passed from one to the other, though it usually remains within the family.

Candles

Candles are an indispensable part of witchcraft, and witches must always have access to them. Fortunately, the candles are cheap and can easily be found anywhere. They also attract little attention, which makes it easy for witches to practice their magic. There are even dedicated branches of magic for candles and the spells you can do with them. Candles can summon deities, for manifestation, and several other spells. They represent the element of Fire in spells and rituals, and they often symbolize the God and the Goddess in Wicca.

Another candle usage is in spell work, where they are utilized to absorb the witch's energy and then release it as the candle burns.

Chalice

A chalice or a goblet is not necessarily a tool for spell making, but many witches believe that it is a symbol of the Goddess or her womb. It is also symbolic of the element of Water. There are certain similarities between the chalice and the Holy Grail, though, in witchcraft, its symbolism is much different. It does not represent the blood of Christ but rather the womb of the Goddess. It can be filled with wine or water and passed around a group of witches practicing magic, or it could be wine offered to the Goddess.

Cauldron

Despite its somewhat comic use in films and cartoons, a cauldron is an essential tool for witchcraft and spell making. It's used to burn incense and herbs, brew potions, perform water scrying to enhance visions and look into other realms, and make offerings. This three-legged vessel is usually made from cast iron. The cauldron can also hold large pillar candles. Many modern cauldrons are portable and can easily be moved around.

Compass

Acknowledging the four cardinal directions is often a prerequisite for many spells and rituals. Not every witch has an excellent sense of direction, which is why a compass sometimes proves to be integral during spell work. It will help you orient yourself in the right direction so you can harness the right energies and align yourself properly.

Crystals

Crystals are another essential item for making spells and performing magic. They hold within them the earth's energy, each with a unique frequency that allows it to vibrate at a different level. Crystals have varying purposes, and you will need to use the ones suited for the spell you are making. Crystals are used for healing, while others are used for manifestation. Generally, crystals are also great for meditation. Remember to choose one depending on your intentions for the spell work. You should regularly clean your crystals, and more importantly, recharge them either during a full moon or by burying them in the earth while you sleep at night.

Clothes

There isn't a uniform dress code for doing magic, but witches have personal preferences with their attire when performing spells or rituals. Many believe that colors can affect the flow of energies and how they move, which is why many witches wear black during rituals to keep from scattering any energy or causing distraction. You could also wear ritual clothes like a cloak, robe, or mask so you can achieve the right mindset to perform the magic you need.

Jewelry is common during rituals and spell casting, especially for Wiccans. Many witches and practitioners wear jewelry displaying pentacles or other pagan and religious symbols during rituals and spell casting, and they can also be worn during everyday life. In several forms of Wicca, people wear a necklace with a circle to signify the circle of rebirth.

Divination Tools

Divination is one of the essential practices for witches, and you will need certain tools to practice divination. Start with a crystal ball, oracle cards, tarot cards, scrying mirrors, and pendulums because each of these will have a very important use when performing divination. You will use these items to look into the future, receive messages and information from deities and mystical powers, confirm your intuition about something, and communicate with your guides on a psychic level. You won't necessarily use those tools; most witches don't; they just use one or two. You just need to find certain divination tools you can master and keep practicing until you perfect your gift with those tools.

Spear

While a spear is not an essential item for spell casting, it is still one of the more popular witchcraft tools for many Wiccans. It is believed to represent the Horned God in rituals that invoke him. This is why several traditional Wiccan rituals require this spear.

Herbs

We've mentioned herbs several times already, and that is because they play a very important role in spell casting. Herbs hold the energy of the earth, each with its unique signature and importance. Herbs can be used in many spells, and they can also be used as incense, in smudging, and for kitchen witchery, and in baths and other self-care rituals. It's always a good idea to have a mortar and pestle if you are going to be working with herbs because they will help you crush the herbs and mix them into powders.

Pen and Paper

You will notice that several spells require the witch to write something down, such as your dreams, desires, or emotions you want to get rid of. This is why you must always have a pen and paper nearby for such cases. You will burn papers if you're doing certain spells, and for others, you will do nothing with the paper. So, be mindful of the paper you get for your spells. Some kinds burn faster than others, while other types shouldn't even be burned. As for pens, you should have a few on hand and include various colors because color magic demands so. Witches recommend charging your paper or pen by waving them through the smoke of the incense, preferably during phases where the energy coming from the moon is at its peak.

Incense

We also mentioned incense several times since it is another basic spell-making item you always need. Incense is a powerful tool that can focus your energies and intentions for manifestation. You can also meditate with incense since it helps channel your energy and focus your thoughts and feelings. Incense is also crucial for cleansing rituals and blessings of a space. You can use it to purify yourself and other members in a magic circle. Incense often comes in different forms and smells. It can be sold as cones or sticks, and the varying fragrances might serve different spells or rituals.

Pentacle

Many people confuse pentagrams and pentacles, and the difference can be confusing. The pentagram is a five-pointed star, and the pentacle is the same, but the star is enclosed in a circle. Other symbols might be engraved on the pentacle, but the pentagram is the one most commonly used. It is a protective amulet often made from wood, but it can also be made from wax, metal, or clay. Some witches believe the pentacle represents the Earth element, and it is used on altars for different purposes like blessing items and tools. It is also used to charge objects, like crystals or chalices.

Offering Bowl

Some witches follow a religious path, and they offer sacrifices or offerings to their deities. If you're going to do that, you will need an offering bowl in which to place those offerings to the Gods and Goddesses.

Lunar Calendar

Finally, any witch who wants to cast spells during the moon phases must have a lunar calendar, also known as an almanac, with the detailed phases of the moon. This will help you prepare the spells and rituals you want to perform throughout the month because, as we mentioned earlier, you should not cast spells haphazardly. Each spell needs to be cast at exactly the right time, so you get the desired result.

Preparing for the Spells

The most powerful magical tool is you. Spells are about your energy, belief, and willpower. This is why you have to prepare yourself spiritually and mentally for spell casting, so you achieve the desired outcome. Here is what you can do.

1. Preparations

Timing: You can't just wake up from your afternoon nap and start concocting spells. You need to prepare first, and you have to be in a certain state of mind. The first thing you need to do is select an appropriate time for the spell. Go through your lunar calendar and select the best time of night to cast your spell, when the moon's powers are at its peak and ready to be harnessed. The more accurate your timing, the more potent your spell will be.

Location: The second thing you need to think about is the location you will prepare your spell. Sometimes, the success of the ritual will depend on the location. You have to find a place where you can be undisturbed so you can focus and channel your energy, somewhere calming. It is also preferred that rituals and spells are done outdoors where the setting is natural and near the earth. Sometimes it might not be easy to find an outdoor location. If so, try to get as close to nature as you can. Finally, make sure you have enough space for your ritual.

Review the Spell: The first time you read a spell should not be the first time you perform it. Take the time to review the spell and familiarize yourself with it. Don't memorize it, but it should come to you naturally and flow smoothly. You do not want to become flustered or forgetful while crafting the spell or ritual because this will affect the outcome.

Prepare the Tools: After reviewing the spell and understanding the tools, you'll need, collect them, and prepare them for the ritual. Don't wait until the last moment because you don't want to waste your window when it comes to lunar alignment. Prepare the tools and space for the ritual beforehand and make sure everything you will need is within reach.

2. Self-Care

You are the most important magical tool, and you need to prepare yourself for whatever rituals or spells you will engage in. Before casting spells, remember to eat light meals and snacks in the hours before. You don't want food to weigh you down or make you feel sleepy. You need to be centered and focused so you can get the best results from your magic and spells.

Also, meditate. This will help clear your mind and put you in the right mindset to practice magic. Take the time to achieve this by meditating and centering yourself. Dampen the lights, put on soothing music, light candles, and close your eyes. Focus on ridding yourself of any negative energies and find your center. Take your time with this because meditating can be the difference between a successful ritual and a failed one.

You could also try a cleansing ritual to purify yourself. Revert to the cleansing ritual we mentioned earlier in the book and perform it before casting spells. Fill a bath with water and essential oils and natural salts. They will help purify you and cleanse you of negative energies.

3. Cleansing the Space

Before you cast spells, cleanse the magical space you'll be working in. This will help get rid of any negative energies and unwanted frequencies. You can use natural earth elements to help you with the cleanse. Find sea salt, rock salt, and a few fabric bags. Mix the salts in the bags and place them in the four corners of the room. Say out loud that you are cleansing this space of any negative energies and forces. You need to visualize that happening, not just say it. Picture the negative energies and frequencies, leaving your magical space.

You can burn incense to further purify the location. Use a smudge stick like cedar or Sweetgrass. You just light the stick until it burns and then blow on it. The smoke will keep coming, and you can use it to smudge the entire space and cleanse it all--move in a clockwise direction with the stick. Like with the previous ritual, visualize and imagine the negative energies escaping your magical space.

4. State of Mind

Your state of mind makes a difference in the ritual and how things will turn out. You need to be in a conducive mindset because it will help you reach your goals. Mental discipline is key here, and meditation can help you reach that level where you can be so focused on your goals and visions that all else disappears. You need to keep a positive mindset in the days and hours leading up to your spell casting. You already know the time when you will cast your spells, and, until that day comes, you need to immerse yourself in positive thoughts.

Avoid worrying about your spells and rituals' success because this is the easiest way for them not to work. During the spell, you need to practice a heightened state of awareness; your mind needs to be conducive for magic and at peak energy so you can attain the required results. You need to access your subconscious while remaining conscious and focused on the moment. It might sound complicated, but with enough training and discipline, you will get there.

Your positive thoughts need to continue even after the spell is cast. If you let your mind wander to negativity or self-doubt, you could ruin everything for which you have worked. The best thing you can do is to not think about a spell you've performed; if you do, try to keep positive thoughts. As a distraction, you can prepare for your next spell.

Part 2: Practical Moon Spells

Chapter 4: Love Spells

By now, you will understand the different lunar phases and their significance, the moon and the energy and power you can harness through it, and how the different phases can be utilized to your advantage if you make the right spell at the right time. We then explored the tools you can use to cast spells and practice magic. Now it is time to get into practicalities and how to cast such spells.

The first spells we will be exploring are love spells. From Goddesses to witches, love spells have been around for millennia, used to draw someone's love and attention or get rid of it. A love spell is simply an enchantment you cast during the proper lunar phase so you can change your fortunes when it comes to love. No matter the problems you're facing romantically, this spell can help you. A love spell could help you start or resume a relationship with someone who you have been dreaming about for months. It could also help you get over a breakup or move on from a past relationship.

A love spell can be cast to attract a new lover or make someone fall in love with you, though you need to be careful with the latter. A love spell can also strengthen the bond of love you have with your partner and help progress the relationship to the next level--those who want to get married but feel that their partners have cold feet, take note.

With love, spells, potency, and efficiency make a lot of difference. Unless the spell is cast perfectly, you will not get the results you want. If you're doing it wrong, it doesn't matter if you cast the spell 20 times; it still doesn't work. So, follow the instructions presented to get the results you want every time you cast a love spell.

Tips

For love spells to work, you must focus on your intention before you do anything. You can't just utter the words and hope for the best; you need to believe this will work, and you need to fully know the consequences and outcomes of your actions because this is how they can come to be. You can't be sleepy, distracted, or under the influence while performing a love spell, or any other spell. You need to have your wits about you, and you must know your senses. Your intentions need to be genuine and of good nature. You are trying to change your future, and you cannot try such a feat on a whim.

It's important that you also determine the desired outcome of the love spell before you cast it. There is no such thing as casting a general love spell and hoping good things will come to fruition in your life; your goals need to be focused and clear so you can reach them. The best advice with a love spell is to focus on your own emotions and feelings rather than trying to influence other people's feelings because you would likely not want the same done to you, but if you are comfortable influencing others, then you can move forward and work on the love spell as intended.

Another thing to remember with love spells is your feelings. You can't have two lovers in mind when you're casting this spell; you have to be certain of your feelings. Your feelings cannot fluctuate, or else you risk the spell not working. There has to be certainty and conviction in every step you take, or else things might not go your way.

One final thing to always remember with love spells specifically is to manage your expectations. You must believe in your love spells' outcome, but that does not mean you shouldn't have realistic expectations. The spell won't drop prince charming in your lap the next day, nor will it have Hollywood's most eligible bachelor fall in love with you. If the spell aims to make someone fall in love with you, you need a preexisting relationship with that person and some prior connection, or it won't make sense for the spell to work. The goal of the spell, would be trying to bring forth more abundance and love into your existing relationship rather than trying to change someone's feelings or perceptions so they will notice you.

Lunar Phase

Spells cannot be cast randomly; they need to be cast at specific times following the lunar phases so you can get the desired outcome. The best time to cast a love spell is during a Full Moon, where the moon's energy is at its peak, and you can harness and channel those energies, but this does not mean you cannot cast a love spell at other times during the lunar cycle, though the nature of those spells will vary. To attract new love, you should cast a love spell during the Waxing Moon phase. To end a relationship and get rid of your feelings for someone, then your spell should be cast during the Waning Moon phase. The New Moon is also a great time to cast spells to manifest love and other positive things you want in your life.

Now that you understand when you can cast your love spells, it is time to learn how. Again, remember to focus on your intentions and believe in the positive outcome of your magic. Do that, and those spells will change the course of your future. Before you work on your love magic, remember to cleanse yourself and your magic space of any negative energy and vibrations. This is not an optional step because you need your space to be clear of any hate or other negative emotions so you can start the rituals with a pure soul and in a cleansed space.

Spell 1: Facilitating Love

The first love spell we will discuss is a New Moon ritual to manifest love and abundance in your life. If you have an existing relationship with a person and want to bring forth more abundance and love in that relationship, this is the spell to cast. This ritual starts by creating a sacred space that is calm and relaxing, so you need to declutter and cleanse the space first. The tools you will need are a pen or pencil and paper. Light a candle at your altar and smudge the place with sage or use essential oils. Then you need to think about the relationship that you'd like to manifest in your life. Think about the qualities and how you want your partner to be, and write those things down along with your intentions.

Then, place a rose quartz crystal on the paper because that is a powerful magical tool for manifesting and attracting love, and it also promotes self-love, which you need for this ritual to work. Now that you have written your intentions and goals, it is time to meditate on them. Close your eyes to the relaxing effects of the candle and think about and visualizing your intentions. The more you believe in them, the better your chances will be of them manifesting and coming to fruition.

Spell 2: Attracting Love

This ritual is like its predecessor, with minor differences that will help you attract new love. This spell is the best cast during the waxing moon phase, which is the perfect time to attract new things to your life and draw more love and affection that will change your life for the better. You will need a piece of paper and a pen with red ink. You will also need a candle, but it has to be a red one.

Start by lighting the candle and slowly delve into a deep meditative state, focusing on the candle's smoke. Clear your mind of negative thoughts and focus on what you want to attract during this lunar cycle. Then, write down on the piece of paper what you want to happen in your romantic life and what you want to attract. The candle wax would already be dripping at this point; let it drip onto the piece of paper after you have written the things you want to attract romantically. The last thing you need to do is to bind the spell, and you can do that by calling on the Goddess – usually Venus for this spell – and asking her to lead someone into your life because you deeply love them and are attracted to them.

After you're done with the spell, sit down and meditate for a while and keep visualizing this person entering your life. Focus on your intentions and believe that good things are coming your way.

Spell 3: New Romance

There is always hope for a new romance, especially with this particular spell. Have a coworker that does not think about you, romantically? This ritual can help change that. You will need a photograph of the person you want to fall in love with you. You will also need blue and red candles and incense, preferably rosewood. This spell is the best cast during a New Moon.

The ritual starts with lighting the candles, blue for luck, and red for love. Light the rosewood incense so you could get into the right mindset and relax before casting your love spell. After relaxing and getting into the right frame of mind, face the picture of your desired lover and kneel before them. Then, invoke the Goddess and express your intent of gaining attention and love from this person. Close your eyes, focus on your intentions coming true and meditate for a while in the same position. Don't think about anything else at that point but your goal and this person falling for you.

Spell 4: Finding the Perfect Partner

This spell utilizes rose petal magic, which can be very potent if done right. It is an easy spell, though you might meet challenges trying to find the right moment to cast it. You will need rose petals to perform this ritual and a body of water like a river or the ocean. This spell is the best cast during the Waxing Moon or a Full Moon, so you can harness the moon's energy and channel it to attract the perfect partner.

The first thing you need to do is think about if that partner is perfect for you. What qualities do you want them to have? Think long about that and visualize the person with all those qualities. Next, throw your rose petals into the moving body of water, asking your guides or deities to bring you true love, as those petals are moving out to the seas or open waters. Repeat this ritual twice, all while visualizing your ideal partner and thinking about your intent.

After casting these love spells, you mustn't obsess with the outcome. This can form negative energies that could jeopardize the outcome of your ritual. Obsessing is never a good idea, and the same goes for when you're practicing magic. A love spell can work if you stay patient and think positively. So, give the spell time to work without losing your patience and trying to rush the results. Have faith and trust that good things are coming your way.

Chapter 5: Fertility Spells

The association between the moon and fertility has been an everlasting one throughout countless civilization. Beyond spiritual beliefs, several studies have also found that the female menstrual cycle is also linked to the different moon phases, which does not come as a surprise considering how the moon is the representation of the female deity. Some of the most important spells and rituals you can practice during the lunar cycle are associated with fertility.

Witches practice fertility spells during the moon phases for different reasons. Some seek to enhance their fertility and increase their chances of getting pregnant, others try to make sure that their newborn is healthy and well, and some try to secure safe delivery. Fertility spells are not just associated with childbirth. Fertility can also mean abundance and bringing more good and wealth into your life. This section will explore spells that you can practice promoting fertility and abundance in your life using magic and sacred rituals.

Fertility Ritual

The first ceremony we will be talking about is a moon fertility ritual. It is best done during the waxing to full moon phases, though you have to sync those with your own body as a female if you are trying to increase your fertility and get pregnant. If so, then this spell is the best cast two weeks after your cycle begins. If this spell is cast to increase a man's fertility, then the spell's timing does not matter as much. As for the time of day to cast this spell, it is the best cast during the early evening hours when you are at your most creative and focused.

Tools: You will need lots of incense for this moon fertility ritual. Get sandalwood incense since it is said to promote mental fertility, and peach incense because it promotes physical fertility and abundance. Don't forget to source an incense burner naturally so you can move around freely with the smoke if you need it.

Deities: This will depend on your set of beliefs and the deities in which you believe, but for Wiccans, there are particular deities you can invoke for this fertility ritual, including Ishtar, Freyr, Brigid, and obviously Diana.

To prepare for this ritual, cast a magical circle. As always, cleanse the magical space and the circle before you begin the ritual. You need to get into the right mindset before starting, so also meditate if that helps you relax. Cleanse your mind of any negative thoughts and feelings. Visualize your negative vibrations dissipating slowly from your body and focus on your intentions. Then, light the incense and state your purpose for this ritual. Invoke the deities that guide you and declare out loud to them your goal and what you want to carry out through this ritual.

As the incense burns, imagine its smoke filling you and touching you, especially the parts of you that you want to be fertile. This ritual dictates you implore each of the four directions, starting with the east. Reach out to the four elementals and implore them to help make you fertile and fill your life with joy. Then, after you've implored the four elements in the four directions, lie down on the floor facing north, stretching your arms and legs. Call out to the deities you invoked here and ask them to bless your loins and make you fertile. Relax and feel the moon's energy wash over you to fill your body with power and fertility.

Kneel before your altar and bless the food you have there. You should have a salad with cucumber and carrots, and olive oil and garlic dressing, a banana, and flavored tea. This food should be consumed after the ritual not to fill you up, but to give you energy. Imagine the food you're consuming, filling the infertile parts of you with energy, and changing that part to be fertile as you slowly eat.

To conclude this ritual, ground yourself and meditate. Find your center and close your circle as you slowly focus on your intents and visualize yourself becoming fertile. If this spell's purpose is to make you fertile and have kids, engage in sexual activity within a day of finishing the spell so you can see its effect coming to fruition. Remember to have faith and believe this spell will work. Hopefully, you will soon become fertile, and your blessed loins will bear a child.

Fertility Spell

This next spell is a very easy one to cast because its ingredients and concept are simple. As always, the most important part of this spell is you. The energy you bring into this spell will determine whether it will work, so be mindful of the vibrations you bring and watch your feelings and intent. This Wiccan fertility spell requires a pen, blossom powder, jasmine spiritual oil, Adam and Eve spiritual oil, and a red female figure candle, plus a plate.

Start by writing your name on the bottom of the female figure candle. After you've done that, place the candle on the plate and then add the jasmine and Adam and Eve spiritual oils and the blossom powder to cover the candle. With the mixture covering the body, rub it with your fingers over the female figure's stomach. Then, stand the candle up on the plate and light it.

You can invoke your deities at this point and ask them to bless your loins with fertility so you can have kids. Close your eyes and meditate, visualizing this spell working and your infertile body changing to become fertile. You must put positive energy into this spell, or else it would not work. Do not obsess over the spell's outcome, but believe that it will work, and you will find fertility and abundance. Don't dwell on negative thoughts, or else you might jeopardize the success of the fertility spell.

Full Moon Spell

This is a full moon fertility spell you can do to promote fertility and ask the Goddess to help you bear a child. It needs to be performed on a full moon, as we've mentioned, preferably on a Monday around 7 pm or 7:30 pm. This spell takes a few more steps than the previous one, and you will need more ingredients, but don't let that deter you. Just focus on finding each ingredient, and then we'll walk you through how you can use them.

Tools/Ingredients: You will need a pen or pencil and paper, three taper candles (pink, blue, and green), cinnamon oil, sandalwood incense, a bowl of soil, a small box or jar, and a baby blanket--if you already have a baby, you could use their blanket for this spell, which would make it more potent and efficient.

Before you cast the spell, you need to first cleanse yourself. Take a ritual bath with natural oils, especially cinnamon oil. This will help rid you of any lingering negative energies and cleanse your body. After you're done, prepare all your tools and ingredients and start your spell.

Cast a magical circle and light the incense. Invoke the deities that guide you or the Goddess. You must take your time with this step because these deities will come to join your circle and guide you on this journey. They will hear your prayers and help you reach your goals. Take the fresh soil you've gathered and sprinkled it around your circle, honoring the Goddess and asking her to provide you with fertility. After that, cover your altar with the baby blanket and pray to the gods and goddesses, declaring this is the blanket with which you will cover your little one.

Then, you need to take the three candles and place them next to one another, with the green one at the center, blue to its left, and pink to its right. As you do this, keep praying to the deities and declare these are the candles that will light your womb. Next, take the green candle, lather it with cinnamon oil, and picture your child. You need to see them in your mind's eye. Picture yourself pregnant with them and then giving birth. Visualize holding the fruit of your loins in your arms and hold on to that mental image. Put the green candle back in the center of the table.

Light the other two candles and use them to light the green candle. As you do so, declare your intent to the Gods and Goddesses. Pray to them and ask them to give you a boy or a girl, pink for girls and blue for boys. After you finish chanting and praying to the deities, take the pen and paper and write down the names you want for a boy and a girl. Put both papers inside the box or jar you've prepared earlier and placed it in front of the green candle. Then let the candle burn down until it extinguishes itself and then place the box somewhere safe. Finally, engage in a sexual relationship with your partner and wait for the spell to work.

As with previous spells, remember not to dwell or obsess about the success of your fertility spell. Place your faith in the spell and let it disappear from your mind. If you can't help thinking about it, make sure your thoughts are positive. Let go of negative thoughts or fears.

Safe Childbirth Spell

Another very important spell that witches cast for fertility concerns the newborn's health and well-being. No one has full control over such matters, and unfortunately, it happens often that a newborn is in poor health and needs help that others cannot give. This is why safe childbirth spells are common, and they can help you to increase the chance that your child is born in good health.

To do this spell, you won't need many items. You need a green candle with a pine scent and an apple. Remember this spell is done after conceiving, and you do it if you are concerned that your child might be born with an inherent problem or in bad health. Take one half of the apple and rub it over your belly and then close your eyes and meditate. Visualize the sickness and bad health being drawn out of your womb and the child growing within it like poison from a wound. After you've done so, take that bad half of the apple and bury it in the earth far away from your child's room.

Eat the other half of the apple and picture your child being born and living a healthy and happy life. You can light the pine-scented candle as you eat the apple; they have healing effects, and pine is linked to fertility and Mother Earth.

Wash up and cleanse yourself. If a tree grows from the buried apple remains, then your child will grow strong and will connect to the earth. Again, the most important part of this spell is your energy and ability to visualize your child living a happy and healthy life, free of disease and suffering. So, focus on your intent and keep a positive mindset throughout this entire spell.

Chapter 6: Money and Career Spells

Money and career spells are very important for witches who want to find wealth and satisfaction in their lives. These spells are great for those who would like a break in their careers or the chance to advance and grow professionally. The spells that we will discuss in this chapter can help you find wealth and attract money and the career opportunities you have been waiting for all your life. If you want a raise or a promotion in your current job, these spells could also help.

You might think casting a spell to get money is hard but thinking so is what makes it hard. You need to believe this will work. Channeling the flow of money into your life is just channeling certain energy, and once you connect to your inner power and tap into the moon's energy, there is no energy flow out there that you cannot control. So, work on your belief and visualizing the money you need for that new house or car.

Full Moon Money Spell

The full moon is the time when the moon's power is at its peak, and you can harness that power to your advantage to channel money into your life. There are other times when you can cast money spells, but we will be talking about a full moon money spell for this first ritual. Wait for this part of the lunar cycle to come by so you can get the most from the spell, amplifying its effects. This spell is naturally cast overnight so you can harness the moon's energy. It is practiced best if you can see the direct moonlight coming through your window. It can work if it is shrouded in clouds, but try to wait until the light is unveiled for most potency.

The tools you need for this spell might sound complicated, but the spell is a lot easier than it sounds. You will first need a mirror and don't worry about mirrors being bad luck. They are ordinary objects that can be charged with certain energies. More important, they can help you amplify the moon's energy to make your spell even more powerful. Find a small round mirror, though any shape will work. You will then need a permanent marker and cinnamon oil (you can use ground cinnamon also for this spell). You need three coins; they should be gold coins, but other types might work. The last thing you need for this spell to work is a green pouch that is spacious enough to accommodate the coins and the mirror.

To start this spell, you need to find a clear view of the full moon. If you have a small private garden, that will be ideal, but if you can be bathed in the moon's glow, the spell will be potent. Gather all your ingredients and sit facing the moon. Close your eyes, calm your mind, and relax. Try to get into a meditative state to clear your thoughts. If you are indoors, open the window to get air. Put the mirror on a surface where the moonlight can hit it.

With the marker, draw the symbols of wealth and prosperity on the mirror's center—there are several Wiccan symbols you can use here, like the key and the number 3. Then, take the cinnamon oil or powder and dip your finger in it and then draw a circle around the symbol of prosperity you have drawn. Don't drown the mirror in oil or powder; use just enough to draw a circle. The next step is to put the three coins you've prepared evenly on the circle of cinnamon oil or powder, marking the symbol of prosperity. Close your eyes again and delve into a meditative state as the moon charges your tools with its power. Focus on your intents and be very specific here.

Focus exactly on the things you want with as much specificity as possible, whether it is determining the amount of money you need or the type of promotion. Immerse yourself in the feelings you will have when you receive that money and visualize it happening. In this immersive state, imagine the moon's light and power washing over you, and then channel that energy and everything you want into the mirror. Open your eyes, invoke the deities, declare your intents, and ask them to guide you to get the money you need.

Finally, take the coins and drop them consecutively into the green pouch, and then slowly put the mirror on top of the coins. Close the pouch and keep it somewhere safe where you can look at it whenever you want until your desires manifest. You can repeat this ritual on the next full moon using the same ingredients, but use fresh cinnamon the second time around.

Spell to Get a Job

There comes a point in every person's professional life when they want a job. This can come early on or later in your career, but it always comes, and you may need a little help to make things go your way. This spell should only be performed after you've submitted your resume or applied for the job. It can help you get the job that your heart desires, but you need to be specific with this spell to get the desired results. As always, believing this spell will work goes a long way toward it working.

They need a sharp tool, like a knife or a pin, green and red candles, and milk. This Wiccan spell starts with writing the company's name you want to work for on the large green candle. Then, on the red candle, carve *Tiwaz*, also known as the victory rune, which is like an arrow facing upward, besides your full name.

This spell should take place on a Thursday. Burn both candles on a Thursday evening for half an hour, and then snuff them out, but don't blow the candles out. Leave a bowl of milk overnight, outside your house, as an offering to the Gods and Goddesses. Repeat this ritual every Thursday at the same hour, but let the candles burn for 15 minutes. Repeat until the candles burn out, or the job is yours.

New Moon Promotion Spells

A person often is passed over for promotions they deserve, which isn't fair but happens, nonetheless. Climbing up the corporate ladder is not as easy as you might think, and you may need magical help. This spell is used to help you do just that, and it can help you get that elusive promotion.

This is a new moon spell, so you have to wait until a new lunar cycle casts it, which makes sense considering that you are looking for a new beginning, which is what this lunar phase is associated with. Prepare your altar for this magical ritual and cleanse your space of any negative energies. Find gold glitter and place it in a jar on your altar as you picture yourself getting the promotion. Clear your mind and focus only on climbing up the corporate ladder and achieving your professional goals.

After that, find the stairs and climb those stairs with the jar held in your hand. You need to have faith and confidence while you are climbing those stairs because this step represents you climbing the corporate ladder and attaining your professional goals. While climbing the stairs, declare your intentions, and invoke the deities to guide you until you get that promotion you are after. After reaching the top of the stairs, put down the jar of gold and meditate. Visualize yourself getting the job and working on it until you achieve success and prosperity.

New Moon Money Ritual

This is a ritual to attract money, and it needs to be done at the start of a new lunar cycle. Wait for the new moon and prepare the items you need for this ritual to work. It is simple, and all you will need is three green candles. The ritual starts by lighting those three candles as you dive into a contemplative mood and meditate. Focus on wealth and the amount of money you want to attract to your life.

Then, invoke the deities or your guides and pray to them. Pray to them and ask them to fill your life with money and abundance, all while focusing clearly on your intents and the money you want to invite to your life. Remember to always focus on a specific amount, don't be vague. Keep burning those candles every day while declaring and renewing your intents until the money manifests. Repeat the prayers every time you light the candles and do this until the candles are gone or until the money manifests.

Ritual for Performance Reviews

Everybody dreads a performance review. It feels like your work is under the microscope, and the review might also decide whether you qualify for a raise which makes it a very important step to a healthy career. You can cast this spell to get the most out of your performance review you often dread. This spell is the best cast a day before the time of the review.

This ritual starts with you putting on the exact clothes you will be wearing for the performance review. Ground yourself and calm your mind while sitting in a chair. Put meditative music on in the background. Close your eyes and reflect on your journey since you got the job or since the last review. Think about your accomplishments and the things you want to mention to prompt your superiors to give you a raise or a promotion. Write those reasons and accomplishments down on a piece of paper. Then, place the paper in your pocket because you will be using it for later.

Wearing the same clothes, right before your performance review, find a quiet spot to sit down and look at that paper. Close your eyes and visualize yourself, getting the raise or the promotion you want. You need to feel the positive energy of those accomplishments and the things you've done wash over you and flow into your body. You can then call out to your guides and ask them to guide you during your review to get the things you have wanted and worked so hard for. This will give you the guidance and positive energy you need to go into that performance review and do great things.

Money and career spells are only as good as your belief and confidence that they will work. You need to invest in your faith in the deities and the guides and trust they would guide you in finding the money and abundance you're looking for, and career advancement and prosperity. Visualization is essential for these spells to work. You have to see yourself getting those things and believe that you can achieve them. Money and career spells are not just about believing in the magic, but it is also about believing in your worth and that you deserve to have those good things happening to you.

Chapter 7: Manifestation Spells

The moon can be so powerful that it can help you get the things you want most in life. If you learn how to harness the moon's energy and power, there is much you can do. The moon can help you improve your health, find love, and find a better, more fulfilling career. The lunar phases can be utilized to such a powerful effect if you understand what you are doing. This is why you need to teach yourself how to align with the different phases and manifestations so you can get everything your heart desires. It takes time and practice, but when you master it, you will have much greater control over your life and the things that manifest within it.

To commit to manifesting with the moon, in this chapter, we will explore manifestation spells that can help you work with the natural forces of the moon and live in sync with all the moon's phases. Be very patient with manifestation because this is a process, and it takes time. Being one with the moon's energy and manifesting the things you want in life isn't something that will happen overnight, and you need to understand that. The best time to perform manifestation spells is when the moon is full.

Full Moon Ritual

The full moon is a time for manifestation and seeing your plans coming to fruition. It is the most powerful time of the lunar cycle and represents completeness and being fulfilled. To manifest with the full moon, we will look at the powerful Full Moon Ritual.

Mindset: The first step of this full moon ritual is to get into the right mindset. This is a part of the lunar cycle when you need to be quiet and reflective, waiting for the actions and intentions you've set earlier to come to a realization. Start by calming your mind and find serenity in your magical space so you can harness the immense power present during this lunar phase. Light a few candles, smudge your magical space with incense, and relax and clear your mind. You cannot manifest with the full moon unless you are in the right mindset.

Reflect: Reflect on the past during this ritual. What has happened over the past few weeks? Are your goals and desires manifesting and coming to fruition? Should you do something different? Look for opportunities for self-improvement and success so you can change the upcoming days. Think about the roadblocks you've faced and the challenges that have slowed you down. This is how you can work on a plan to overcome these challenges and turn things around over the next lunar cycle.

Declaring Intent: By this point of the ritual, know what has worked for you and what has not. So, write down the things slowing you down and the things you want to happen. Take the paper on which you have written down the obstacles blocking your path and burn it or flush it down the toilet. This will help you overcome these obstacles and reach your goals in the future.

Go Outside: Some people call it a moon bath, and it is a peaceful time basking in the full glow of the moon. Either way, go outside and sit under the moonlight. Let it wash over you with its energy and power. It will help you spiritually and physically since the moonlight provides several benefits to our bodies, just like the sunlight. It will also help you relax and focus on your intentions for the next lunar phase.

Dance: There is nothing like dancing to help you manifest and align your powers and energies to those of the moon. Dancing is therapeutic and can help you release any negative energy you still have, so it is a cleanse of sorts. So, dance! It will make you feel better and more relaxed. Dancing under the moon will help you find your spiritual base.

Water Ritual

The second full moon ritual we will discuss is a moon water ritual that can help you manifest, clear your mind, and open your heart. This ritual starts with a mason jar you fill with tap water and then screw on the lid. The tools for this ceremony are simple, as you can see, and it can be done easily, though you need to believe it will work to get the best results.

Take the water jar and put it outside under direct moonlight, and let it stay there overnight--make sure that the lid is on so the water does not become contaminated. Then, after putting it outside, take time to think about and focus on your intents for the next lunar cycle. Think about the things you want to accomplish and how you will do that. In the morning, you can reclaim the jar to do one or more things with it. You can drink a little of the water every day, and every time you take a sip from the moon-blessed water, remind yourself of your intents and goals. This water has the power of the full moon in it and can be very potent.

You can also use this enchanted water to bless your magical tools, especially your crystals. The crystals can absorb magical energies if bathed in moon water, and this will help amplify their powers, making them more potent in your upcoming rituals and spells. Some people use this blessed moon water on their skin as a beauty element. They add it to an oil or cream and then place the beauty product on their faces every day.

This ritual can help you align your energy with that of the moon because the moon's power will accompany you constantly with that blessed water, so use it wisely and keep reminding yourself of your intentions and goals. Manifesting with moon water can bring you closer to your goals and dreams.

Wishes Manifestation Ritual

This ritual is all about harnessing the power of the full moon to manifest your wishes and bring them to life. You will need paper, a pencil, candles, and a box of any shape or material. Start this ritual by listing your manifestations. Let the Goddess guide you, and her power and energy usher you into writing down your manifestations, so you can see them coming to fruition.

Light a candle to start this ritual and focus your thoughts. Let go of negative thoughts in your head and forget about past pains and troubles. Focus on the now and the present moment, releasing other thoughts lingering in your head. Take a moment to think about the things you want to release or get rid of and what you want to attract and invite into your mind and soul. Then, write down on the paper the things you want to invite into your life over the next lunar cycle. List everything and focus on making your intentions pure and realistic. These full moon wishes could be fulfilled by the next lunar cycle, so channel your energy and focus on your intents while writing those wishes down.

Then, place the piece of paper with your wishes in a box or a jar-- any container will work here. Take the box or jar and place it outside in the moonlights so it can absorb its energy and bask in the immense power coming from the moon. Like with the previous ritual, in the morning, reclaim the box or the jar and take it into your house. Put it somewhere where you can see it every day. Ideally, it could be your altar, which is already a magic space regularly cleansed and charged.

But you could also place the jar on a counter or your nightstand if you wish. Every night, before you go to bed, consider your wishes you want to manifest and think about why you want those things. This will help you realize and manifest those things in the upcoming lunar cycles.

Cleansing Ritual

You can't manifest with the different lunar cycles unless you cleanse yourself and your space. The key to manifestation and realizing your goals is ridding yourself of negative energies and frequencies, which is the purpose of this ritual. You will need a few simple ingredients for this one: incense or herbs like rosemary and juniper. The purpose of this ritual is to use the smoke coming from the burned incense or herbs to purify your home from dark energies, and the full moon is the perfect time to do that. Performing a cleansing ritual like this one during this part of the lunar cycle can purify your home from bad frequencies and lingering negativity.

Light the herbs or incense and then move around the different rooms in your house with the smoke to purify each area as you go. Take advantage of this cleansing ritual to release anything you don't want in your life, too, and get rid of darker thoughts that are no longer serving you and are just slowing you down. Let the moon Goddess guide you in this cleansing ritual as you waft the smoke around the house. Go where you feel the energies are darker or negative and declare out loud that you cleanse this space of any negative influences. Once you're done wafting the smoke, open the windows and let the moonlight wash over your rooms, recharging energy and driving any negative influences out. This helps regenerate your home's energy and leaves you with a cleansed living space free of old energies and filled with new ones.

New Moon Ritual

The new moon is a time for new beginnings, the start of a fresh lunar cycle. You can move away from the past and think about the future, looking forward with positivity instead of focusing on your shortcomings and errors. In this phase of the lunar cycle, you need to consider what you want to come into your life and what you want to let go of. It is the perfect time for reflection and rests and planning for the future. A new moon is not the time for action like other lunar phases, so make no rash decisions. Here's how you can perform a new moon ritual.

Prepare a Space: The first thing you need to do in a new moon ritual is to prepare a sacred space in which you can reflect and rest. So, declutter and get rid of anything that you don't need in your magical space. Next, cleanse your space using incense or oils.

Cleanse Yourself: When it's a new moon before you can start the ritual, you need to cleanse yourself. So, after cleansing your space, take a ritual bath with natural salts and essential oils. Let the water wash away your negative energy and cleanse your body of any impurities. Dim the lights and relax in your ritual bath, meditating and relaxing. You've earned your rest, and this is the time where you can relax in preparation for what is to come.

Ground Yourself: An integral part of this new moon ritual is grounding yourself, and the best way to do that is to have all four natural elements present. They will help ground your magical space and keep you too grounded. The candle represents fire, a water bowl with salt represents the ocean, incense depicts the wind, and natural herbs represent the earth. These elements have a calming effect and can keep you focused and relaxed.

Turn a New Page: Once you're grounded, focus on the connection to the greater energies at work. Tap into the moon's energy and try to harness it. When you feel grounded and connected to the moon and its power, you can then turn a new page, both literally and metaphorically. Take paper (or journal) and start writing. Don't force anything; just let the writing flow out of you and clear your mind as you do so. Write everything you're feeling and thinking at that moment. Declare your intentions and the things you'd like to experience in the weeks to come. When it comes to writing your intentions, be specific because this is how you manifest them. The clearer your intentions are written, the easier it would be for you to manifest them.

Ask for Guidance: After reflecting on your goals and dreams and declaring your intentions, it is time for the final phase of this ritual, which is receiving spiritual guidance. Turn to your deities and guides and ask for help. You can use oracle cards or other magical tools, but it's important to form this connection with your guides so you can trust you are on the right path. Whatever deities or guides you believe in, pray to them and invoke them for guidance and help.

The last step of this ritual is to close your eyes and visualize. Meditate and concentrate on the things you want, and focus on turning a new leaf and starting over. See your intentions manifested and see the things you want in your head. Whatever you want in your life during this lunar cycle, the new moon is the time to think about it and visualize it manifesting. Trust the process, have faith, and it will manifest for you.

Chapter 8: Protection Spells

Whether you want to protect yourself against harm or your loved ones against any evil they might meet in life, protection spells are what you need. This spell is very important when we live where people's intentions and energies are not always pure. This is why you need to have charms and spells in place to keep you and everyone you care about from being harmed.

Energy Cleanse Ritual

The first ritual we will discuss for protecting your home is energy cleanse. It will combine most techniques we have mentioned and help to rid your magical space and the rest of your home. of negative energies and frequencies. You will need several magical tools here, starting with a besom or a broom.

First, you will take the besom or broom and sweep the negative energy out of your house. You must focus on intent, which is clearing the house of any negative energies. Go to every room in the house, moving in a counterclockwise direction, and sweep all the negative energy toward the front door. Start with the ceiling and then move to the corners but don't let the broom touch the walls or floor; you are sweeping energies out of the rooms, not actually sweeping dust.

Declare your intent as you move from one room to another, sweeping away all negative energies and declaring that they are not welcome in your space.

After you're done sweeping all negative energies from your space, you will perform a smoke cleanse. You need to burn sage and then move around your house with it to bless the rooms and cleanse any residual negative energies. Like with the sweeping, move in a counterclockwise direction and focus on every room's four corners because this is where negative energy often dwells. The smoke of the sage will help you get rid of any lingering energies, and more important, bless your house with love, wealth, and abundance. Visualize these more positive energies covering your home as you perform this part of the ritual and imagine the negative energy being replaced with the positive one.

After this, you will use a bell to renew the energy of your house. We mentioned earlier how bells could help ward off dark energies; they can also bring peace and harmony to your home, which is always required with such a ritual. While moving with a bell around your home, circle in a clockwise direction to bring in energy. You can chime the bell three times in each room because three is a sacred number. As you ring the bell, declare your intent, and say what energy you want to attract, always repeating positive phrases and chants.

We're toward the end of the ritual now, and this next part is about anchoring and preserving the positive energy you have invited. You will do this by using crystals, which contain immense energy and can stabilize your house's energy levels, keeping them at the level you need and wish to be surrounded by. To anchor the energy in your home, place a crystal in every room; the type of crystal will depend on the energy and vibrations you wish to keep--crystals have different powers, and you need to put ones that will serve the purpose of the room. You could put a black crystal next to your home's entrance to cleanse any negative energies and offer protection. In your bedroom, you could add rose quartz to promote love and intimacy with your partner. As you move to each room, placing the crystals, move in a clockwise direction, and visualize the energy you wish to infuse with the crystals. Focus on your intent and visualize the crystals carrying this positive energy and anchoring it in each room.

The last step of this ritual, which is to infuse your house with positive energy further, is to go around every room again and draw a pentacle. The pentacle is a symbol of all major elementals, and it can add lots of positive energies to your house. Using a wand or a crystal, move around the rooms in a clockwise direction one last time and draw the pentacle on the doorway ceiling of each room, invoking the deities and the elementals in the process and asking them to offer protection to your home and to bless it.

Doing this ritual, you will have managed to cleanse all dark and negative energies from your home. You will have replaced those with positive energies that will last and offer protection for you and your loved ones.

Protection from Enemies

We always fear pain and torment, whether it is physical or emotional, but unfortunately, it sometimes follows us around no matter what we do, which is usually because of the evil in people and places. With a little help, you can protect yourself and your loved ones from such torment using this Dark or Waning Moon spell--toward the end of the lunar cycle, right before the new moon. This spell is to protect you and the people you care about from an enemy or someone who may wish to do you harm.

To start this spell, make sure you are using a dark altar. Place two candles, one on each side of the altar--one of them needs to be black. After casting your circle, you need to write on the black candle the name of your enemy or the person bringing negative energy. Then, invoke your deities and ask them to help you and protect you and your loved ones. Dip the black candle in the juice of the dieffenbachia plant, which you should prepare beforehand. This juice has the power to numb the tongue, which is to stop your enemy from speaking bad things about you and your loved ones. While dipping the candle in the plant juice, ask the Goddess to stop your enemies from speaking evil about you and request that their tongues be numbed.

You also need spider webs for this spell because you will next roll the candle in the webs and ask the Goddess this person be caught in a web of their deceit rather than harm you or your loved ones. Light the candle after writing the person's name on a piece of paper, and keep praying to the deities to protect your family from all evil and cause this person to face the consequences of their actions. Then, burn the paper with the name, placing it in the black candle's flame, collecting the ashes as they appear. The ashes need to be sprinkled at night in a location where you are certain your enemy will walk, perhaps by their home or place of work. Finally, light the second candle, blue or white, and meditate. This candle signifies the peace and harmony bestowed upon you and your loved ones now that you are safe from your enemy's evil.

Dark Moon Protection Spell

This is another Dark Moon protection spell, which means it needs to be done on the lunar cycle's last day. This spell utilizes a charm bag to protect whomever you want. You can use the spell to protect your children as they grow, your lover at work, or even yourself from evil forces. In simple terms, a charm bag is a pouch that encloses enchanted items that manifest a certain intention, in this case, protection. A charm bag has to be kept on you or worn for some time to see results. While charm bags have often been depicted negatively in movies and TV shows, often claimed to be used by witches to harm others, they are used positively in real life and can help you keep your loved ones safe.

This spell is ideal for the Dark Moon because this time of the month is associated with the Dark Goddess, the Crone. She is known by many names such as Persephone, Lilith, or Hecate. She is the protector and the wise woman, which is why this is the perfect time for banishment and protection spells. In short, this spell can provide you with protection against the darkness out there because it is associated directly with the Dark Goddess.

The best time to perform the spell is during the moon's waning phase or on the Dark Moon itself, right before the New Moon. Try to perform this ritual on a Saturday. You will need a few things for the charm bag, but most of these are easy to find. You should have a maple leaf, a charm bead, black ribbon, lock of hair, Himalayan salt, dragon's blood oil, lavender, nettle, sage, black tourmaline, and a black pouch or piece of cloth in which you will add the ingredients. This spell is performed over two steps, and the second one is a consecration ritual, for which you will need a black candle and incense.

Prepare everything as you sit by your altar, meditating, and getting into the right mindset. Focus on your intent and prepare to cast the protection spell. Cast a magical circle and fill the pouch with the ingredients we've listed (except for the bead and ribbon). Conjure and focus on your intention to be protected or to protect someone you care about from harm. With the pouch filled, thread the protection bead around the black ribbon and seal the pouch with it.

For the second part of this ritual, light the black candle, and invoke the Goddess. Pray to her and ask her to offer you protection and consecrate the charm bag so you can use it to protect yourself or your loved ones against all evil in the world. You can create a chant or use a standard one, but make sure it delivers the true meaning and implores the Goddess for her help in consecrating the charm bag so you can use it for protection. Visualize the protective energy emanating from the pouch and imagine that energy is shielding you or whoever you're making the spell for from any dark energies and all evil. When you're done, praise the Goddess, and snuff the candle, concluding your ritual.

This charm bag should be carried with you or the person you've made it for. It can be worn, put in a bag, or even tucked into your pocket. Just don't move without it, or at the very least, never keep it out of your sight. Remember: nobody else should touch the bag! If that happens, you must perform another ritual to consecrate it. At the end of every lunar cycle, recharge your protection charm by either dosing it with moon water or leaving it under the moon overnight.

Black Salt for Spiritual Protection

Black salt is one of the most common magical ingredients used to offer spiritual protection for your soul and home. It is incredibly useful and efficient in countering the effects of the negativity we encounter in our daily lives. From toxic relationships and exhausting working conditions to your demons and overthinking, negative frequencies are more common in our lives than we would like to admit. This is where black salt comes in. It can absorb the negative energy coming in from all around you and pluck away the dark vibrations troubling you.

So, how do you make it? You need one thing: black pepper, activated charcoal powder, fire pit ashes, or black food coloring. You use one of those with coarse sea salt to make your black salt. To make a more potent black salt, you can also add ingredients like rosemary, cinnamon, lavender essential oil, or cayenne powder. Combine the salt with those and then use the moon's power to charge this combination. You can leave the mix under the light of a dark or a full moon to increase its efficiency and heighten its powers.

Now that you have your black salt, it is time to use it! There is no specific rule on how you should use it, so you can do so however you please. You can sprinkle black pepper around your home to protect you and your loved ones from any darkness or evil. You could also put some in your car to protect you from road trouble or in a small jar at your office to keep away toxic coworkers and the trouble that comes with them.

Chapter 9: Banishing Spells

The last spells we will be discussing in this part is banishing spells, which can be used for a variety of essential purposes. A banishing spell is simply used to get rid of any negative influences in your life, whether those are people or thoughts and feelings you have been struggling with. A banishing spell could relieve you of the pain of a traumatic experience that has long haunted you. You also cast a banishing spell when you want to end a toxic relationship or friendship doing you more harm than good or want a fresh start and let go of the past with all its pain.

Full Moon Release Ritual

While banishing spells are customarily cast during the moon's waning phases, some can be cast during a full moon, as this release ritual. This ritual focuses on tapping into the moon's energy and its natural alignment with our moods and cycles. Our moods change with the change of lunar phases, and your energy levels do, too. This release ritual will help you tap into the full moon's power so you can get rid of anything slowing you down or causing you pain in life. You will need a pen and paper, sage or oils, and candles.

To start this ritual off, you need to cast your magical circle, but first, cleanse your magical circle of any lingering negative energies that might be impeding the ritual. You can put on soothing music to get into the mood and prepare yourself mentally to go through this ceremony. Clear your mind of all thoughts and focus your energies. You can also burn candles and incense to help you focus and channel your energy. The candles will also cleanse the space of dark vibrations and negative energy. Visualize all bad energies seeping away from your body and leaving you to meditate calmly under the moonlight.

Then, ground yourself and take control of your body and breathing. After meditating, you must learn of the moment and of how you are feeling. Think about the things you would like to release from your life and why you wish to do so. It could be a job causing you pain and exhaustion or a relationship weighing you down and affecting your life negatively. Whatever it is, write it down on a piece of paper and declare your intent to get rid of this negative effect on your life. Then, sign your name on the paper and date it. Finally, close your eyes, and declare to the universe you are releasing whatever it is that is troubling you from your life. Visualize this happening and have faith that the universe will handle everything.

After that, hold the paper with your hand over the lit candle and let the flame burn away your troubles and release the negativity. Visualize the smoke of the burning paper declaring your intentions to the universe and helping you find peace and harmony. You must end this ritual on a positive note. Meditate and clear your mind of thoughts about the negative thing you have released, and be grateful. Sit in peace and silence for a while, and be grateful for the things you have learned from those tough situations or toxic people. Forgive those that have wronged you and let go of any hatred or negativity you have toward them--this could also mean forgiving yourself for any pain you might have caused. You've released whatever it is that was troubling you, so there's no point in dwelling on the loss and pain.

Express your gratitude toward the universe for helping you release those troubles and thank the deities for helping you wash those troubles away. Finally, take a ritual cleansing bath to calm yourself and wash away any remaining negativity.

Spell to Banish Negativity

No matter how hard we try, the mind has its way of dwelling on the negative things affecting you. You can try hard to have positive thoughts and not dwell on what's hurting you, but sometimes, the negative thoughts are just too powerful. This spell will help you deal with such problems, and you can banish ideas from your mind.

You need a cauldron, pen, red candle, and two pieces of paper for this banishing spell. You can perform this spell during the waning or new moon phases, but never during the waxing moon. Start by drawing a picture of yourself with the dark thoughts weighing you down. There is no right way to do this because it is up to your interpretations and feelings. Maybe you want to draw a picture of yourself with a black cloud hanging over your head or a picture of someone sobbing. Whatever you are feeling, draw it. Then, take the red candle and charge it with the moon's energy because it will have a healing effect for this spell. After that, light the candle and hold the tip of the picture you have drawn in the flame.

When the picture catches fire, place it in the cauldron. Then, draw another picture of yourself, this time happy and without the negativity weighing you down. Take this second picture and place it under the red candle. Then, let the candle burn out as you visualize yourself releasing whatever is bothering you and enjoying a happier life, all with the moon's light washing over you and recharging your energy.

Four Thieves Vinegar to Banish Evil

This is one of the most popular potions to banish evil and negativity, and its origin dates back hundreds of years. You will need lavender, rosemary, sage, thyme, mint, apple cider vinegar, garlic, and a jar or airtight container for this spell. You should also choose fresh herbs for this spell.

Start by putting the herbs inside the jar and then cover the herbs with apple cider vinegar and close the lid tightly. Store it in a cool and dry place, and give the jar a gentle shake every day for 1 to 1.5 months. Then, take the herbs out of the vinegar, and your potion is ready to use. There are several ways to use the four thieves vinegar, and it will help you banish all evil and ward yourself or your loved ones against the dark forces at work in the world.

You can sprinkle this vinegar around your doorstep to keep dark energies and evil out and to protect your home from enemies. If you don't mind the taste, it can also be used as an ingredient in cooking to provide you with protection and banish all evil around you as you move, plus break spells that might be cast upon you.

Spell to Banish Depression

Stress and depression are the plagues of modern humans. Whether it is the stresses of your daily job or depression from existential crises and not knowing your purpose in life, this spell might just help. You've already probably tried every other approach to making yourself feel better and getting rid of your stress and sadness, and it might just be time to try something different.

For this spell, you will need a black stone and a candle. This spell requires going to a body of running water, preferably during the new or waning moon, so find the nearest stream, brook, or even ocean. Sit down, light the candles, and hold the stone in your right hand. Calm yourself and meditate. Think about all the things weighing you down and causing depression and stress. Channel those thoughts and negative energies into the stone you are holding. When you feel those troubles and pains have left your body and settled into the stone, toss it into the water and chant. Declare to the Goddess and the universe you wish for those feelings and thoughts to have left your body, and you wish them to be replaced with peace, serenity, and happiness.

After doing so, ground and calm yourself, sit and dwell on the feelings you are experiencing, and how good it feels to be rid of those dark thoughts and the depression. Thank the Goddess for her help in relieving your pain. Stay for a while at the body of running water and let the moon's energy wash over you and rid you of any remnants of negativity and depression. Then, blow out the candles, pack up, and go home, believing that your depression is a thing of the past.

Reflective Banishing

We all have people and things in our lives that are a source of constant stress and pain, and they can channel their negative energy towards you so you often find yourself unable to resist being affected by the negativity. This spell is for this situation; it's designed to reflect this negativity at the target, whether it is a toxic person in your life or unwanted spirits causing you a lot of pain. You need a small mirror and something to write with (an oil pencil works perfectly here).

Write down the name of the person or spirit causing you pain and declare underneath the name you henceforth send back and reflect this dark energy. Add a banishing symbol too. Then, carry the mirror around with you until this person or spirit has ceased channeling their negativity your way.

Spell to Remove Curses

This next spell is all about removing curses from an object. If you have an object you believe is cursed, this spell could help. Removing curses often depends on the curse's strength, but you need to try several approaches until it is lifted. Try a purification ritual to remove a curse from an object; you can do that by dipping the object in saltwater and then lighting incense and letting its smoke cover the item -- you can also use holy water instead of incense. If the curse is weak, it will be removed by this simple purification ritual. If it is strong, you might need to do something else.

Until you know exactly the curse on the item, you need to at least limit its harms so you could do a counter-spell. You can do so by putting a copper item on the object since copper is capable of drawing negative energies and maintaining a certain balance of the object's energy. This is a temporary solution, though. Your best chance knows what curse has been placed on this item so you could perform a particular ritual or cast a certain spell that works with this specific curse. Copper can only draw negative energies for so long, and it might fail so this is not a long-term solution to this problem. If you do encounter a cursed object, follow a certain order. Start with the cleansing ritual and pray it works and removes the curse. If it doesn't, try to learn as much as you can about the curse and understand what exactly it can do. Until you do so, use a coin or any other copper object to dampen the effects of the curse and reduce its harm.

Spell to Banish Danger

This is a very important spell for banishing dangerous people you might have crossed paths with and feared for your life or that of your loved ones. It will help you banish the danger and protect everyone and everything you care about. You will need a red ribbon, poppet (doll) to represent the person (or persons) that are dangerous, a black candle, and myrrh incense.

Cast your magical circle and light the incense and the black candle. Put salt water on the poppet and declare your intentions towards this person. You want them to stay away from you and your loved ones, so declare it and bless the poppet for this chant to work. Then, hold the doll in your hand and visualize it bound by a silver net, representing the dangerous person being bound from ever hurting you. After that, use the red ribbon to tie the poppet up tightly, making sure you bind it so it cannot do you any harm.

After binding the poppet, charge it by chanting to the Gods and Goddesses and honoring the elements. Declare that you wish this poppet and who it represents to be bound and their harm banished from you and everyone you care about. This marks the conclusion of the spell. Open your circle and take the poppet and bury it. Bury it under a waning moon, bury it far from your home, and put a heavy rock over its burial place. This will help banish the danger this person brings and will protect you and your family from their evil.

Spell to Remove People from Your Life

The next spell we will discuss is to banish unwanted people from your life. You will need sea salt, black and white candles, a picture of yourself, and a quartz stone to perform this spell.

Cast a circle of the sea salt and put the quartz stone, the white candle, and your picture inside it. Bless the white candle and demand it protects only you from any possible harm. Then, light it. After that, take the black candle and bless it to absorb all negative energies that might affect you. Light this black candle and place it outside the salt circle and let it burn out. This will help protect you from any negative energies and keep that person away from you until they are removed from your life.

Spell to Banish Alcohol Addiction

Struggling with alcohol addiction is one of the worst challenges a person can find themselves in. Unfortunately, it happens often without you even noticing. You tell yourself it will be just a glass or two to take the edge off or relax after a long and stressful day, and you could soon find yourself addicted to that numbing sensation that alcohol gives you. In these tough times, you could do a spell to banish this addiction and help you stop drinking alcohol.

For this spell, get around a dozen pieces of small paper, a pen or pencil, black string or cord, a glass of water, amethyst crystal, and an empty bottle of your favorite alcohol, but it needs to have a lid, and wash it before this spell. Before you begin the ritual, think about why you want to stop drinking alcohol. Whatever those reasons were, write them down on a piece of paper, separately. You need to be honest with yourself here, so write down the reasons as they are, whether you're hurting the people you love, affecting your job, or anything.

Next, cast your magic circle as you usually do and meditate for a while. Calm yourself and clear your mind; you must have untroubled thoughts for this ritual to work. Then, pick up a piece of paper and read what is on it out loud and then declare its opposite also aloud. For instance, if the paper said, "I argue with my wife a lot because I drink alcohol," then you need to affirm its opposite and say, "I don't fight with my wife as much now because I stopped drinking alcohol." Visualization is key for this ritual to work. You need to imagine yourself freed from the burden of alcohol abuse and without a care on your mind now that you are sober. Believe that the things you are reading out loud are true, and they will come to be.

Think about how it would feel if it were true, and you were free from this addiction and healthy, leading a better life. Take the piece of paper you've read and put it in the empty bottle. Then, pick up another piece of paper and repeat the process. Once you have finished them all, put the lid on and close the bottle with the papers inside. Take the black string or cord, tie it around the bottle's neck, and do three knots (remember the importance of the number 3). Next, take the glass of water, let the moonlight shine on it, washing it over with its energy. And drink water. Visualize this water cleansing you and purifying you of the need for alcohol.

Finally, take the crystal and put it in your hands, and sit in the moonlight. Feel the light covering you with its power and let it flow from you to the crystal. Meditate on getting rid of your alcohol addiction and becoming sober, all while holding the crystal. Then, declare it to the universe; say you are not a drinker anymore, and it shall be true. Close the circle and meditate for a while. Then, take the bottle and get rid of it; you can bury it in the ground or just throw it away. After the ritual, remember to carry the crystal with you. If you ever feel the urge to drink alcohol, drink water, and visualize as you did before, just believe it will work.

Spell to Banish Negative Influences

Finally, we will discuss a candle banishing ritual to help you get rid of negative influences in your life. For this, you need a black candle and a candle holder, salt, a carving tool, like a pin or sharp knife, black or white pepper, and an anointing oil of any kind.

Start by sprinkling the salt in a counterclockwise direction to form a circle around yourself. As you sprinkle it, visualize the salt-forming a protective shield around you and your magical space to protect you from any dark forces. Think about your banishing spell's goal and what you wish to get rid of, be it is a person or a feeling. Then, declare your intent by carving this desire into the candle, like wishing to lose your anxiety or exhaustion or wanting someone never to cross your path ever again. It is also a good idea to carve a banishing sigil or symbol into the candle.

When you're done, use the oil to anoint the candle and also sprinkle it with salt. Then, place the candle in the holder and light it while declaring your intentions out loud. Let the candle burn out as you sit down next to it and meditate, visualizing your desires coming to fruition and whatever you want out of your life being banished. After you are done, break the circle and forget about the spell.

Part 3: Other Ways to Work with the Moon

Chapter 10: Moon Water, Crystals, and Oils

By now, you understand many spells that you can cast with the moon's power, but there are still many ways through which you can harness that power and use it to your advantage. The energy that comes from the moon over the lunar cycle can bless many items and charge your magical items with energy. In this chapter, we will explore other ways to use the power coming from the moon, whether it is to create moon water or to consecrate your crystals and work with oils. These techniques can be done separately, or they can be done together to maximize your harvesting of the moon's energy.

Moon Water

We gave detailed instructions in a previous chapter about how to create moon water, but that is not the only way it can be crafted. Some prefer to make moon water during the new and full moon phases, only to be used in special magical rituals and at specific times throughout the lunar cycles. Others make moon water during the waxing or the waning lunar phases. It all depends on your preferences, connection to the moon, and the time you think is ideal for working on this ritual. Here is a simple guide on how you can make moon water, but you can follow a different approach if you please.

1. Preparing the Container

The first step to making moon water is preparing a container reflective of not just who you are as a person but also what you are trying to attract. If you are trying to attract wealth, you can use a more expensive vessel. You could also use a mason jar of any kind, but it needs to be charged with your intent and your goals for the next lunar cycle so you can use it to the maximum efficiency.

2. Charge the Container

While don't do this step, it is beneficial if you do. Charging the container before you perform the moon ritual can help ward off any negative energies that might be lingering around and draining your energy or infusing you with negative vibrations. You can use crystals for this purpose because they have healing effects and can help protect you from negative energies and unwelcome influences.

3. Put the Container Under the Moonlight

With the container ready, fill it with water. You should use a jar or container with a lid to avoid having anything contaminating your moon water. Then, take the jar and put it under the moonlight during the phase you feel will be best to charge your water--ideally, it should be a full or a new moon. While you should put the jar under direct moonlight outside, if you live in an apartment and this will be complicated, you can put the container by a window.

4. Retrieve the Container

After leaving the jar overnight, retrieve it in the morning with your newly-charged moon water. Keep your moon water with you because there are many ways you can use it.

Water Elemental in Rituals: The first way you can use the moon water is in your magical rituals. Put moon water in a chalice, place it on the altar, and it can be a representation of the water element during your rituals. You can use this chalice of moon water to call the quarters, too.

Offerings: Moon water can be an offering to the deities. It is the perfect offering to the deities you invoke, and it can help you summon their guidance and blessing. Put some of it in a bowl along with flowers or petals, or whatever offer you think your deities would appreciate. After that, present the offering to your deity with a chant or a prayer of your making.

Blessing and Charging: You can use the moon water to bless any magical items you use during your rituals and spells. You can use it, for instance, to bless the pen with which you will write in your book of shadows or bless your wand or any other magical items you will use during rituals. Moon water can charge and cleanse your altar and all your magical tools. To consecrate a magical item with moon water, dip a finger in the moon charged water and then draw a pentacle or other magical symbols on the items you want to bless.

Charging crystals in moon water is one of the most common practices for witches as it regenerates and charges the crystals' powers, and you can then use them for cleansing rituals and other magical spells and ceremonies. The combination of crystals and moon water can be powerful if used correctly.

Anointing: Moon water is often used to anoint objects and not just magical ones. For example, you can anoint your money with moon water to promote wealth and attract good fortune. This is because water as an element is often associated with money, as both flows. For such a ritual, focus on your intents and be specific to the wealth you'd like to attract. Imagine the wealth and abundance flowing in your direction, much as water would.

Cleansing: Always remember that moon water can cleanse your home of any negative energies and dark vibrations.

Beauty and Self-Care: A lot of witches use moon water for beauty purposes. You can wash your face with it or add it to beauty products. You can add moon water to your bath to recharge your body and cleanse it while you're bathing. You can also use it in vases with flowers to give your flowers a blessed life.

Promoting Creativity: Moon water is believed to boost and promote creativity. You can clean your workspace with moon water and even wipe your vision board with it. You can use moon water with your chakras to promote psychic abilities and creativity.

These are just ways to use moon water; essentially, you can use it in whatever way you want. From cooking to cleaning, this charged water can give you positive energy and cleanse you of bad vibrations, plus bless your home.

Crystals

Crystals can be used with moon energy to a great effect, but you need to know what crystals to work with and how. The challenge with crystals is that there are many types out there, and you need to select the right kind to work with and in the proper moon phase, or else your intention won't come to manifest. Here are crystals you can use to harvest and channel the moon's energy.

Moonstone

While it may sound a little obvious, the moonstone is one of the best crystals to work with the moon's energy. You don't need a particular color of moonstone; it could be white or even black. The best thing about this crystal is that you can use it to work with lunar energy during all moon phases, so you're not bound to the new or full moons, though its power on the full moon is extremely potent. If you feel that power while wearing it on a full moon and do not like the amount of power you feel, you can put it aside until the moon's next phase with no adverse effects.

The moonstone resembles the Goddess and the feminine energy that comes with her, which is not surprising considering the moon itself manifests the Goddess and divine feminine energy. Use the moonstone to tap into your intuition and channel your gut feelings to help manifest your desires. Whenever you want to align with your goals, and tap into your power, use the moonstone during any moon phase.

Selenite

Selenite is one of the most popular crystals for many witches, and for a good reason. Its power is great, and it's used to do many great things. The name of the crystal is derived from the Moon Goddess Selene, and it is a full moon crystal, so it is best utilized during this lunar phase to make the most out of the lunar energy. There is a certain iridescence to selenite that is like the moon's shine, and it is believed this crystal emanates peace and joy to those who use it.

Selenite can help you process the range of emotions and fears that often manifest with the full moon, which is why it is best used during this part of the lunar cycle. It can neutralize and repel the negative energies that often surround us and bring us down. While this crystal is used to repel dark energies and emit positive vibrations, it could still need cleaning occasionally so you can get the best outcome while using it. You need to charge your selenite under the full moon by leaving it at night to bask in the energy of the moon.

When you use selenite, focus on your intentions and on repelling negative energies. Also visualize this crystal, bringing you joy and happiness and manifesting good things in your life.

Labradorite

There is a certain shimmer of changing color to Labradorite under certain light, which makes it look beautiful and captivating. This crystal has protective qualities and can offer you protection against negative energy and dark vibrations. This crystal is best used during the full moon and is great for manifestation rituals. Labradorite is also believed to be linked to the sun's energy, which gives it an even greater power considering it has both sources of energy linked to it.

This particular crystal is used to help you find balance in your life and in figuring out what is slowing you down. What are you not confronting? What is stopping you from moving to a better place and leading a better life? These are all questions that can be answered using Labradorite since it boosts spirituality and intuition and can help connect you with yourself and your innermost feelings. Labradorite is a crystal of spiritual awakening and transformation, and after using it with the full moon, you can transform your life.

Amethyst

Amethyst is not necessarily used with or linked to the full moon, but it can benefit greatly from its energy. This violet stone vibrates at a special frequency that can be amplified by the full moon. Amethyst can help you overcome the heavy feelings that might be weighing you down, and it can help you navigate your inner turmoil to come out feeling better about yourself and your insecurities.

Amethyst can keep you grounded, boosts spirituality, and puts you in direct contact with your intuition so you can figure out what is bothering you and causing you to feel unhappy. Use this crystal during different lunar cycles, but the full moon most of all, to overcome your insecurities and fears and come to terms with your shortcomings.

Opal

Opal is one of the most powerful crystals you can use during the moon phases. Its strength comes from its connection to the water element, which, as we mentioned several times, is closely associated with the moon's energy. Opal represents purification and is a manifestation of the cleansing of dark energies around your home. Use it to bless your magical tools and altar and to cleanse your home before casting your magical circle.

Clear Quartz

It is believed that clear quartz contains power and knowledge that can bless your moon rituals with powerful protection. The great thing about clear quartz is its versatility, and it is considered one of the most commonly used crystals. You can use it for any purpose, depending on your intentions.

It can be used during the full moon phase to channel your intent toward positive energies and attracting better things to your life. Clear quartz can help you align your energy with that of the moon, so you can declare your intentions to the world and see them coming to fruition.

Moon Oil

Moon oil can increase the power of your intentions and channel certain energies. You can carry it around to repel dark energies and cleanse yourself. Moon oil has herbs and oils blessed with the lunar energy and can help you harness that energy.

To make moon oil, you can choose the oil you like best or believe will fit most with what you need the oil for. If you plan on using moon oil on your skin, it might be worth getting skin-friendly oils and won't irritate. If that is not your intent, then you could use any oils you want to work with. For the intents of this part, we will use grapeseed oil and sweet almond or avocado oil. You can add essential oils like rose or jasmine oil. Add herbs to the mixture--you can choose herbs you think will help you harness the moonlight. Use a small bottle to combine the mixture and use it whenever you need it.

After you put everything in the bottle, add small crystals too to charge the mixture with even more potent energy. Leave the bottle under the moon overnight to charge during any of the moon phases, perhaps the full moon for the greatest power. Collect it in the morning as you would with moon water and use the moon oil however you please.

Chapter 11: Moon Goddess Rituals

In this chapter, we will explore rituals you can perform to honor the Moon Goddess. As you now know, she has been known by many names across various civilizations, all having their ways of honoring her. To this day, several religious traditions still honor the Moon Goddess and conduct rituals in her honor. Some must be done during certain phases of the lunar cycle where her presence is most noted, and others during any part of the cycle.

Drawing Down the Moon Ritual

This is a powerful and beautiful Wiccan ritual to invoke the Moon Goddess. The witch casting this spell invokes the Goddess into herself, drowning into a trance-like state, to speak the words of the Goddess and relay her commands. This ritual is best practiced during the full moon or right before it, and it is best done outdoors so you can be in direct contact with the moon's energy, but if that is impossible, you can do it indoors but make sure you are in a clear view of the moon.

There is not a single right way to do this ritual, and different witch will have varying approaches. It will depend on your personal beliefs and how you generally practice your magic. You will need a cleansed altar for this ritual, so start by clearing the magical space of all negative energies and evil spirits. After cleansing the place with sage or crystals, stand before your altar, facing the full moon, and cross your arms. While in this position, invoke the Moon Goddess. You can use whichever phrasing or chanting you are comfortable with. Just pray to and invoke the Goddess's presence into your sacred magical space.

Raise your arms and move your feet to be shoulder's width apart. By opening your arms like this, you are welcoming the Goddess into your mortal vessel. You will feel your energy fluctuating, and power will surge into your body, which is fine because this is the Moon Goddess entering into you. Speak from your mind on behalf of the Moon Goddess. Declare your presence and your intent and identify yourself as her. There aren't exact words you should chant here; just say what you believe that the Goddess represents and feel her power course through your veins as she takes your body. Honor her and declare your loyalty and undying gratitude to the Goddess, as one should.

To conclude the ceremony, meditate as you feel the power dissipating and the Goddess leaving your body. This is the time to be in a contemplative mood and think about this wonderful thing you have just experienced. Lower your arms to mark the end of the ritual and close the magic circle. You can expect to have heightened powers over the next few days, which is normal; you had a Goddess within you. You might also have sharpened psychic abilities for a few days, so try to look into your future and focus on your intent and the things you would like to invite to your life. The more focused you are, the more you can tap into any residual power that might be in your body and use it to your advantage.

Invoking Artemis (Full Moon Ritual)

This second ritual we will be talking about is invoking the Goddess of Hunt and the Moon Artemis; you will perform this ritual on a full moon. It is similar in objective to the "drawing the moon" ritual because it aims to draw the deity to occupy your body and speak through you, but this one is geared specifically at the Goddess of the hunt. Artemis was believed to be the protector of virgins and all that is chaste, and the forest and wild animals. She was a huntress unlike any other, chaste, beautiful, and pure, also known as the eternal virgin never touched by man or god. This ritual is to honor and pay tribute to her.

For this ritual, you will need a white candle, moonstone crystal, olive oil, mugwort, tarragon, wormwood; you can use only one herb, a combination, or all three. You will also need to prepare shamanic music for the ritual. You need to get into the right mindset before you start this ritual because you are inviting the powerful Goddess Artemis into your body, so you have to be ready. Start by cleansing yourself so you will be receptive to such a powerful deity. Take a ritual cleansing bath to cleanse yourself and become pure to welcome the purest of the Goddesses.

Next, your magical space needs to be cleansed to welcome Artemis. Use smudge or oils to cleanse your magical space, starting at the corners. After cleansing yourself and the location, it is time to start your ritual. Dim the lights, light the incense, and let the candles burn too. Put on shamanic music to prepare your mind and soul and help you dive into a focused meditative state. Cast your magical circle after preparing all the items and ingredients for this ritual.

While listening to the music and enjoying the incense and the setting, allow yourself to dive into a deep meditative state and drift off to a different time and space. Imagine yourself in Artemis's favorite location, a forest in ancient times where trees are everywhere, and wild animals roam freely. Visualizing these scenes is important because it makes for an inviting setting for the Goddess to make her presence known. Then, anoint your white candle with the olive oil and as you do so, honor Artemis and say a prayer for the Goddess. Dedicate this ritual and the burning of the candle to her purity and wild ferocity. After anointing the candle, you need to do the same to yourself with more olive oil, starting from the bottom and moving to the top.

While anointing yourself, it is time to invoke Artemis. You can say words of your choice here, but make sure they are from the heart and carry the honor and veneration that such a Goddess deserves. Invoke the Goddess and ask her to occupy your body and use it as a vessel to bless you with her energy. Call out her name and honor her with the descriptions and titles passed across generations. Then, sprinkle the herbs over yourself and around the candle, honoring the Goddess. Anoint the moonstone, too, and carry it with you. You can wear it as a pendant or put it in your pocket; just make sure it is on you because this crystal represents your connection to the goddess and will ease her passage into your physical form.

Now, it is time to dance! Get up on your feet and dance wildly and freely as the ancient priests did in honor of Artemis. This is the best way to honor the Goddess's pure energy and wild nature, and you need to dance until you can't dance anymore. When your energy has drained, lay back on the floor and let Artemis's energy wash over you and charge you. Slowly sit up once you feel you are blessed with her powers and break the circle. Ground yourself and center. Think about the experience of being one with the Goddess of the hunt and what that means.

You can prepare an altar for Artemis to have her always present with you, blessing you with her ferocity and purity to face whatever you face in life. Set an altar for her with herbs and a white candle, and offer a tribute to Artemis, such as moon water or another magical item.

Full Moon Ritual for Diana

We talked early in the book about the Goddess Diana and how she was considered the triple Goddess and a manifestation of the moon. This ritual is to honor her and to honor the moon's divine feminine power. Diana has often been considered a representation of fertility and feminine power, and she is often invoked in rituals promoting childbirth and relating to women. This ritual is not to invoke Diana to occupy your body but to honor her and form a connection with the Moon Goddess. This is why this is done when the moon is at the peak of its power.

Start by setting up your altar. You don't have to cleanse your altar or space here, but it is often recommended that you do so to connect with Diana clearer and purer. Start with a cleansing ritual, then write down your desires and intents for the future and prayers for the Goddess of the moon on a piece of paper. Take this paper (or cloth) and tie it to a tree. Ask the Goddess to protect you and your loved ones as she protects animals and anyone who worships her and believes in her powers.

Then, back at your altar, continue praying to Diana and ask her to fulfill your wishes and help you find happiness and joy in life. Light a white candle on your altar and offer a bowl of moon water or milk to the Goddess as an offering. Visualize the Goddess helping you get what you want and blessing your life and the life of those you care about. Have faith that Diana can help you get the things you want and meditate on her presence during that full moon. Thank the Goddess for her presence and honor her before you break the magical circle.

Wiccan Esbat

For Wiccans, the Esbat is when they meet on a full moon to celebrate it and honor the Moon Goddess and other deities. They practice magic and express gratitude for the deities that have guided them over the previous lunar cycle. There are approximately 13 Esbats during a year, corresponding to 13 full moons. The Esbat is a time of spirituality and is used to channel the moon's energy to cleanse yourself and achieve your goals. It is also a time for honoring the deities and manifesting their blessing and energies.

While the Wiccan rituals for the sun (Sabbats) have certain meanings, this is not the case with the Esbat. It is about connecting with the moon's energy and using it to change and better your life. This is why there is no right way to practice magic during the Esbats. You just do what your gut feeling tells you and honor the moon and the Goddess; however you want. It can be as simple as going to your backyard during the full moon and meditating under the moonlight and visualizing good things happening.

So, how do you go about a Wiccan Esbat? The most important thing you need to focus on at first is your intention. The Esbat is all about plotting a goal and performing the ritual to promote that goal and honor it. Whether it is to honor the deities, connect with the moon, or to ask the Gods and Goddesses to help you with a personal dream or desire, Esbat is the time to do it. Just be specific about what you want so you can make the most out of Esbat. While Esbats are traditionally performed on a full moon, you could perform the ritual on any part of the lunar cycle if it coincides with your goals-- remember we said phases work better for protection spells while others are more suited toward wealth or abundance. So, whatever you want from Esbat, write it down and consider your lunar calendar to find the ideal moment.

Next comes the preparation. You have now defined your goals and what you want to accomplish through the ritual, and you have a time on which you will perform it. After that comes the research. Understand what you need to do for Esbat to work and the ingredients you will need for this spell or ritual. Is it a manifestation spell? Or do you want to attract wealth or love? Perhaps you wish to protect your loved ones against evil and dark energies or promote your fertility so you can conceive. Whatever it is, research the spell and the ritual and prepare the magical tools and ingredients you will need to make it work.

Finally, perform your ritual. As we mentioned, there isn't a specific way to perform the Esbat or a particular objective, so do as your heart tells you. It is not a bad idea; however, to follow practices like cleansing your magical space and yourself so you can correctly honor the deities and perform a proper ritual. Meditate on your intents and visualize them coming to fruition, and you will have made a successful Esbat.

Chapter 12: Creating Your Own Unique Moon Rituals

In this final chapter, we will explore ways through which you can make your unique moon rituals. The beauty of moon spells and rituals is there isn't any handbook on how they must be performed. There are just guidelines and tips to help you on this spiritual and majestic journey, and this leaves a lot of room for improvisation and adding your unique touch to make the rituals and spells more aligned with your beliefs and practices. You don't have to buy the ingredients you use for spells and rituals we've mentioned earlier; you could just make your own!

At the end of the day, moon rituals are about finding your voice and working with something with which you are comfortable. Your energy and beliefs drive these rituals and spells and are the reason they work. So, let's dive into things you could do to make your unique moon rituals.

Unique Full Moon Ritual

Considering how the full moon is the most powerful of the lunar phases where the moon is at the height of its power, it makes sense we start with tips and ideas on how you can create a unique moon ritual personal to you and unlike any other.

Personalize: This is a full moon ritual, and for it to work, you need to keep it simple and personal. The purpose of this ritual is to align your energy with that of the moon, and for that to happen, you need to be authentic. Think about the practices that mean the most to you and try to infuse them within the ritual. Do you like dancing? Then why not include it in your full moon ritual? Maybe meditating is more your thing, so incorporate that. The ritual is an extension of who you are and the things you enjoy, so whatever you like, make sure to make it a part of the ritual.

Prepare the Tools: You need to prepare the tools you will use to complete the spell or perform the ceremony. Again, this will also depend on your preferences. Perhaps there are certain herbs or a sage you prefer to use. Or you might prefer essential oils. Select a crystal or a unique stone of importance to you. Put on the music that works best for you and puts you in a meditative mood; it could be heavy metal or African drums. Experimentation is key here. Keep trying different things. They might work, or they might not. The important thing is they are yours and express who you are as a person.

Sacred Space: After preparing the tools you want to use for this ritual or spell, you need to prepare a sacred space to do your magic. There isn't a rule that says a sacred space should look like this or that, but traditionally it should contain an altar. The altar's importance is that it gives this space sacred importance and lets you know that it is special, different from day-to-day objects, and not an ordinary table.

You can choose whatever location you please in your home to prepare this sacred space, and you can decorate it however you want, too. The most important thing is you being comfortable and feeling like you can freely express yourself in this space. Then. Cleanse this space you have created and remove any dark energies.

Get into the Mindset: What separates a magical ritual from any other thing you do daily is your mindset. With your tools and magical space ready, prepared according to your preferences, you need to next meditate and prepare your mind for a deep spiritual connection to the moon. Think about the things you want to carry out through this ritual and why you are doing this. Then, take time for gratitude and appreciating all the things you have been blessed with. Thank the Moon Goddess for blessing your life and giving you many things to be thankful for. Gratitude is a very important practice that makes it a lot easier for you to establish a genuine connection with the moon's energy.

Toward the end of this ritual, you may do what you feel like doing to conclude the ritual. Some witches like to journal and write down whatever they are feeling, whether it is desires or fears. Or you could affirm your intent and declare how you want the next lunar cycle to be. You could also go outdoors and bathe in the moonlight and let its healing energy wash over you. Close your ritual once you feel like it has served its purpose. You can do so by meditating again, saying a prayer to the Goddess, singing or chanting, dancing, or ringing a bell and saying moon salutations.

New Moon Ritual

The new moon marks new beginnings, and it is a time to set intentions and work on manifesting them. During this very special time of the lunar cycle, you can create a home ritual to celebrate, and it could be a new ritual. You can practice it alone, or you could invite friends or other witches to join in on the new moon ritual to make it more potent.

Before you start this ritual, make sure the magical space you are performing it in is beautiful. Again, this will depend on what you find beautiful, so take liberties in decluttering and adding aesthetic elements that make the sacred space look beautiful to you. Get rid of the things you don't need and set up your altar in a pure and visually pleasing way. You can use objects from around your home to prepare the altar or earth elements from the soil around your home. Anything can work if you believe in it. Put these items on the altar and decorate it however you want.

For this unique ritual, you can ground yourself. Grounding is a healthy practice you can do regardless of any moon rituals. Grounding is best done near a body of water and barefoot so you can feel the energy of the earth and the water. Make your way to the water and let it cover you--you could go all into the water or just dip your feet. Breathe deeply under the moonlight and visualize your intentions manifesting. Let the cold water ground you and anchor your mind and body. Think about your desires and imagine them coming to be.

You could then choose to conclude this unique ritual in many ways. You could write or journal like with the previous ritual. Document your feelings during this new moon and what you want to attract, and what you wish to release from your life. Declare your intentions for this lunar cycle and what you wish to experience. You could then take the piece of paper with your desires and bury it in the garden or set alight to it with a candle, letting your desires become known to the universe and trusting that it will guide your intentions. To wrap things up, burn sage of your choosing or incense to cleanse the space after declaring your intentions.

Tips for Creating Your Rituals

The key to creating a unique ritual is to think about the things that feel magical to you and only you. No rule says you cannot use handmade objects or custom tools to perform magical rituals and invoke deities. Customize the spells and the chants however you please. The Moon Goddess will not care which chant you use to invoke her and ask for her blessing if you honor her and pay her respect. So, try different things in your rituals and see what works best for you. Does yoga relax you and put you in a meditative state of mind? Then, by all means, incorporate yoga into your magical rituals and start or conclude the ceremony by practicing it.

Conclusion

Customize your moon ritual so it makes you feel comfortable and at ease. Your connection with the moon is special and can be felt only by you. Different things might work with other people, so don't worry about copying anyone else, thinking about the elements you find magical, and adding them to your rituals. Harness the moon's energy using tools that others may not find magical; it doesn't matter. Magic is what you decide is magical. Experiment with your rituals and try combining new things on the different lunar phases. You might just find spells and rituals that could change your life for the better. Remember that you should never despair when it comes to creating your unique ritual. Some will work; others will not. You need to stay patient and keep experimenting until you find the right combination of items and rituals. It is much more rewarding because you can perform rituals you have made yourself and are personal to you, which could make the spells much more potent and help you achieve the results you want.

Here's another book by Mari Silva that you might like

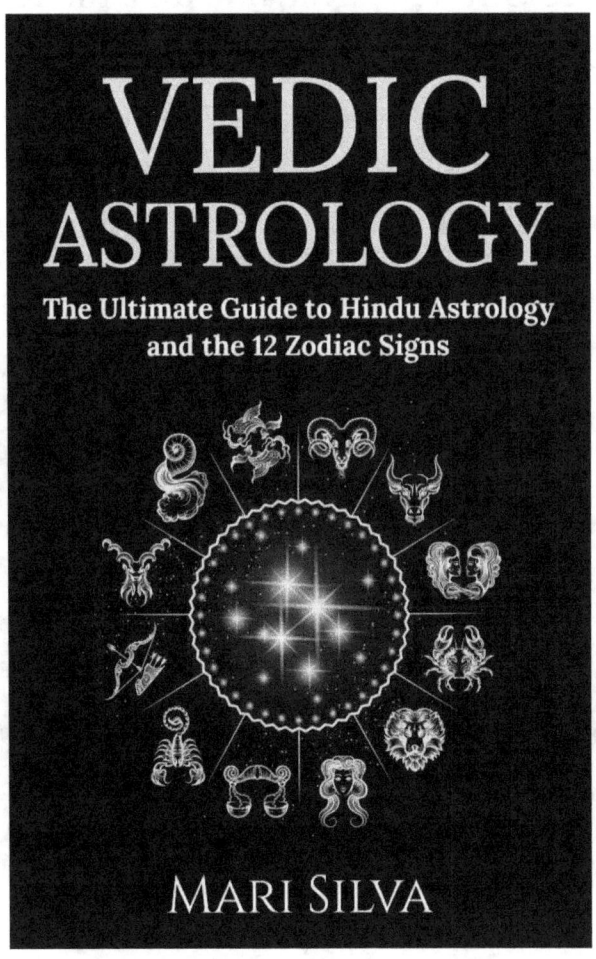

Your Free Gift (only available for a limited time)

Thanks for getting this book! If you want to learn more about various spirituality topics, then join Mari Silva's community and get a free guided meditation MP3 for awakening your third eye. This guided meditation mp3 is designed to open and strengthen ones third eye so you can experience a higher state of consciousness. Simply visit the link below the image to get started.

https://spiritualityspot.com/meditation

References

B. A., H., Facebook, F., & Twitter, T. (n.d.). *10 Lunar Gods & Goddesses You Should Know.* Learn Religions. https://www.learnreligions.com/lunar-deities-2562404

Five Spell-Casting Essentials for Beginner Witches. (n.d.). Exemplore. https://exemplore.com/wicca-witchcraft/Witchcraft-For-Beginners-The-Five-Essential-Parts-of-Casting-Spells

Glamour. (n.d.). *Making "moon rituals" can totally enhance your life, here's your ultimate guide.* Glamour UK. Retrieved from https://www.glamourmagazine.co.uk/article/moon-ritual-guide

How to Prepare For a Spell. (2020, March 9). Wishbonix. https://www.wishbonix.com/how-to-prepare-for-a-spell/

M. A., L., & B. A., L. (n.d.). *12 Ancient Lunar Luminaries.* ThoughtCo. https://www.thoughtco.com/moon-gods-and-moon-goddesses-120395

Moon Rituals for Guiding Intentions. (n.d.). Www.Kelleemaize.com. Retrieved from https://www.kelleemaize.com/post/moon-rituals-for-guiding-intentions

Pollux, A. (n.d.). *The Ultimate Full Moon Money Spell for Abundance.* Welcome To Wicca Now. Retrieved from https://wiccanow.com/full-moon-money-spell/

www.ingramcontent.com/pod-product-compliance
Lightning Source LLC
Chambersburg PA
CBHW062055280426
43673CB00073B/192